HARVEST IN TRANSLATION

The Other Voice

Some Other Books by Octavio Paz

Octavio Paz

The Other Voice

ESSAYS ON MODERN POETRY

Translated from the Spanish by
Helen Lane

A HARVEST/HBJ BOOK
HARCOURT BRACE JOVANOVICH, PUBLISHERS
San Diego   New York   London

Excerpts on page 31 and 70–71 from "East Coker" in *Four Quartets,* copy-
right 1943 by T. S. Eliot and renewed 1971 by Esme Valerie Eliot, reprinted
by permission of Harcourt Brace Jovanovich, Inc.; and by permission of
Faber and Faber Ltd, from *Collected Poems 1909–1962* by T. S. Eliot. Ex-
cerpts on pages 124–25 from the letters of Ezra Pound copyright © 1989 by
the Trustees of the Ezra Pound Literary Property Trust; used by permission
of New Directions Publishing Corp., agents; and reprinted by permission of
Faber and Faber Ltd, from *The Letters of Ezra Pound* by Ezra Pound. Ex-
cerpt on page 96 from "In Memory of W. B. Yeats" from *W. H. Auden:
Collected Poems* by W. H. Auden, ed. by Edward Mendelson, copyright 1940
and renewed 1968 by W. H. Auden; reprinted by permission of Random
House, Inc.

Library of Congress Cataloging-in-Publication Data
Paz, Octavio, 1914–
[Otra voz. English]
The other voice: essays on modern poetry/Octavio Paz;
translated from the Spanish by Helen Lane. — 1st ed.
p.   cm.
Translation of: La otra voz.
ISBN 0-15-170449-X (hc). — ISBN 0-15-670455-2 (pbk.)
1. Poetry — 20th century — History and criticism.   2. Postmodernism
(Literature) I. Title.
PN1271.P39   1991
809.1'04 — dc20   91-4764

Designed by Lisa Peters

Printed in the United States of America

First Harvest/HBJ edition 1992

A B C D E

The Other Voice

Introduction

This book is a collection of essays written in the last few years. The subject of all of them is poetry and its place in our day. I began to write poems very early in life, and began very early to reflect as well on the act of writing them. Poetry is an extremely ambiguous occupation: a task and a mystery, a pastime and a sacrament, a métier and a passion. I wrote my first essay in 1941. It was a meditation (perhaps it would be more appropriate, because of its haphazardness, to call it a disorderly digression) on the two extremes of poetic and human experience: solitude, communion. I saw them personified in two poets whom I read with fervor in those days: Quevedo and Saint John of the Cross—in two of their works, *Lágrimas de un penitente** and the *Cántico espiritual*. I later wrote an entire book, *El arco y la lira*,† which was followed by other essays and then, much later, by another book, *Los hijos del limo*.‡ In the latter I dealt with modern poetry from Romanticism to Symbolism and the avant-garde movements.

The essays in this volume are a continuation of the final

---

*Also called *Heráclito cristiano y segunda harpa a imitación de David* (1613).
†Mexico City, 1956. *The Bow and the Lyre,* trans. Ruth L. C. Simms (Austin: University of Texas Press, 1973).
‡Barcelona, 1974. *Children of the Mire: Poetry from Romanticism to the Avant-Garde,* trans. Rachel Phillips (Cambridge, Mass.: Harvard University Press, 1974).

part of *Los hijos del limo;* they deal with the twilight of the avant-garde and the place of poetry in the contemporary period. We are not experiencing the end of poetry, as certain people have said, but of a poetic tradition that began with the great Romantics, reached its zenith with the Symbolists, and attained a fascinating twilight with the avant-gardes of our century. Another art is dawning.

The contemporary period has been called "postmodern." An equivocal name. If our era is "postmodern," what will our grandchildren call theirs—postpostmodern? It is generally thought that the entirety of ideas, beliefs, values, and practices that characterize what has been called modernity is today undergoing a radical change. If that is true, this period cannot be defined merely as postmodern. Rather, it is simply what has come after modernity: it is something different, something that already possesses features of its own, though they are still in the process of taking shape. As invariably happens, the break was at first noticed by only a very few; however, shortly after the end of the Second World War it became increasingly more visible. One example among many: revolutionary thought had prophesied a great transformation, inevitable and definitive, in the most advanced countries; in none of them did the prophecy come true. Revolutions took place on the periphery of the Western world, but they became petrified almost immediately, turning into bureaucratic despotisms at once pitiless and inefficient.

2

We are now witnessing the breakdown of the two ideas that have constituted modernity since its birth: the vision of time as a linear, progressive succession toward a better future, and the notion of change as the best form of time's succession. Both these ideas were conjoined in our conception of history as a march toward progress: societies change continually, sometimes violently, but every change is an advance. Archetypal time ceased to be the past and a chimerical Golden Age; and time outside of time—the eternity of angels and devils, the just and the damned—was dislodged by the cult of progress. The Promised Land was the future. In the sphere of political action, the manifestation of change was the idea of Revolution; in the realm of art and literature, the idea of New Art, based on a break with the immediate past. Today the future has ceased to be a magnet, and the vision of time that sustained and justified it is disappearing. Along with it, the great myth that inspired so many in the twentieth century, Revolution, is disappearing, too. The twilight of Revolution coincides with the twilight of the artistic and poetic avant-gardes. This is no coincidence: modern art came about as a response—both an echo and an answer—to the French Revolution, which ushered in modernity; thus the fate of modern art became one with the idea of Revolution.

The first part of this little book contains three essays. In the first, I discuss the antecedents of the "extensive poem." This is a poetic form that has had great good fortune in the twentieth century. I do not mean to say that the best modern poems are the long ones. The contrary may be closer to the truth: the intensity of a three- or four-line poem frequently pierces the wall of time. But long poems—those of T. S. Eliot, Saint-John Perse, and Juan Ramón Jiménez, to give three well-known examples—have been an expression of our era and have left their mark on it. The second essay deals with modern poetry and the end of the tradition of the abrupt break. The third is a brief reflection on the ambiguous and almost invariably unfortunate relationships between poetry and the myth of Revolution.

The book's second part examines the function of poetry in present-day society. It concludes with a question: What will be the place of poetry in times to come? More than a description, less than a prophecy, my answer is a profession of faith. These pages are simply a variation—yet another—of that *Defense of Poetry* modern poets have been writing now, tirelessly, for over two centuries.

MEXICO CITY, JANUARY 31, 1990

Poetry and Modernity

Telling and Singing
On the Extensive Poem

A living history is sung
by telling its melody.
—Antonio Machado

What is an "extensive poem"? The dictionary says that to extend is to increase something so that it occupies more space. To extend also means to expand, to develop, to enlarge, to unfold, to occupy greater terrain. In its original and primary sense, extension is a spatial concept. Hence an extensive poem is a long poem. Since in language words come one after the other in a row, an extensive poem is one that has many lines and the reading of which takes a considerable amount of time. Space is time. But how long must a poem be to be considered an extensive poem? How many lines?

The *Mahabharata* has more than two hundred thousand

verses, whereas an *uta,* regarded by the Japanese as a long poem, has some thirty or forty verses. Góngora's *Soledades* has just over two thousand verses, Sor Juana Inés de la Cruz's *Primero sueño* about a thousand, and the *Divine Comedy* some fifteen thousand. On the other hand, *The Waste Land* has only 434 verses, Mallarmé's *Un coup de dés* fewer than three hundred. Long and short are relative, variable terms. The number of verses is not a criterion: a long poem to a Japanese is a short one to a Hindu; a long poem for a twentieth-century reader is a short one to a reader in the Baroque period. Other factors must be taken into account.

Paul Valéry said that a poem is the development of an exclamation. A clear-cut formula, yet one that then requires development. In a short poem, the beginning and the end are fused; there is scarcely any development. In a poem of average length, the beginning and the end are clearly distinguishable, distinct, each possessing its own physiognomy, but at the same time they are inseparable. We read from the first line to the last without isolating the parts. In a long poem, the parts, while not completely autonomous, do exist as parts. We are unable to isolate a part in a poem of average length, because it does not make sense in and of itself; but in an extensive poem, each part has a life of its own. Examples are the Paolo and Francesca episode in Dante's *Inferno,* or the Dante and Matilda episode at the end of his journey through purgatory, or the "Canto on Usury" in Pound's poem.

Poetry is governed by the twofold principle of variety within unity. In the short poem, variety is sacrificed to unity; in the long poem, it attains its fullness of being without destroying unity. Thus in the long poem we find not only extension, which is a relative dimension, but also maximum variety. The extensive poem, moreover, satisfies another twofold requirement, one that is closely related to the rule of variety within unity: repetition and surprise. Repetition is a cardinal principle in poetry. Meter and its accents, rhyme, the epithets in Homer and other poets, phrases and incidents that recur like musical motifs and serve as signs to emphasize continuity. At the other extreme are breaks, changes, inventions—in a word, the unexpected. What we call development is merely the alliance between repetition and surprise, recurrence and invention, continuity and interruption.

Reduced to its simplest and most essential form, the poem is a song. Song is neither discourse nor explanation. In the short poem—*jarcha,* haiku, epigram, *chüeh-chü, copla*—the background and most of the circumstances that are the cause or object of the song are omitted. But in order to *sing* the wrath of Achilles and its consequences, Homer must *tell* the heroic deeds of Achilles, and of the other Achaeans as well, and of the Trojans. Song becomes story, and story in turn becomes song. In its most immediate form, a story is an account of an event, a history. The poem gives us the story of a hero. The extensive poem was originally an epic poem. But the story of a hero is also the story of gods and the history of the relations between the two worlds, the mortal world and the divine. Ulysses, Ajax, Gilgamesh, Aeneas: encounters, loves, and combat with gods and goddesses. The heroic and the mythical fuse: the subject matter of the epic is the valorous deeds of heroes, and heroes are semidivine beings. Is there such a thing as a purely earthly epic, one uncontaminated by supernatural intervention and divine genealogy? It is said that the *Cantar de mío Cid* is a realistic poem. No. Realism is a modern concept, and the poem of the Cid is a medieval text—that is to say, it belongs to an era in which the interpenetration between the real and the supernatural and wondrous was continual. The epic borders at one extreme on history and at the other on mythology. Epic, mythology, and cosmogony in constant interpenetration. The epic poem is first cousin to the religious poem. The religious poem, in turn, soon transforms into the philosophical poem. Examples abound, from Parmenides to Lucretius.

The Christian West introduces a new and twofold novelty. The extensive poem of Greco-Roman antiquity—whether epic, philosophical, or religious—is always objective, that is, the author does not appear in it. Virgil recounts to us the labors and loves of Aeneas. Parmenides tells us what being is and what nonbeing is. Hesiod tells us of the four ages of the earth. In all these poems, the objectivity of the account is not violated; the subject of the poem is never the poet. But in Christian poetry, a new element makes its appearance: the poet himself as hero. The *Divine Comedy* is a poem in which all previous genres—epic, mythical, philosophical—come together, and a story is told. The subject of the poem is not Ulysses' return to Ithaca or the adventures of Aeneas: it relates the journey of a man to the other world. That man is not a hero, like Gilgamesh, but a sinner—and more significant still, that sinner is the poet himself, Dante the Florentine. The poem of antiquity was impersonal; with Dante, the *I* appears.

A great change: the first-person singular becomes the main character of the extensive poem. This was possible because the *Divine Comedy* is an allegory, and that is the second great novelty of the Christian poem. The story of Gilgamesh's journey to the other world is one of the most beautiful and most heartbreaking texts in world litera-ture—a song of the awareness of death—but at no point can that episode be seen as allegory: the journey of the hero to the land of the immortals, however fantastic it may appear to us, is presented as a real, absolutely real, fact. Nor are the stanzas allegorical in which Homer and Virgil tell us of the meetings of Ulysses and Aeneas with the dead. But Dante's journey to three worlds is three allegories in one: the history of Israel is the key to the history of the human race; the story of the Gospels is the story of the redemption of mankind; and the story of Dante is the story of all sinners, the story of salvation through love, which is Christianity.

In many passages of the *Vita nuova,* Dante employs expressions such as "Love said to me," "I saw Love approaching." In other words, he sees Love and hears it; he speaks of it as though it were not a passion but a person. Nevertheless, in the same book, commenting on one of his poems, he writes: "There are those who may be surprised that Love speaks not only as though it were a thing in itself, or an intelligent substance, but as though it were a corporeal substance, which is not true. Love does not exist in itself as a substance. It is, rather, an accident of a substance." To understand the sense of this passage, the reader must know that, according to medieval doctrine, there are intelligent and incorporeal substances, like the angels; substances without intelligence, like the material elements; substances animated by an animal or vegetable soul but not possessed of reason; and finally, substances that are corporeal and intelligent, human beings.* Although Love is not an angelic spirit or a demon or brute matter, neither is it a person. What is it, then? It is an accident of a corporeal and intelligent substance; not a person but something that happens to a person—a passion, a feeling. Yet Dante describes this accident, which lacks form though it is born of the

---

*See André Pézard's note to *Vita nuova* xxv (Paris: Nagel, 1953).

vision of a form, as though it were indeed a person. That is, he makes of love a personification. Later, he explains that endowing love with human attributes is a privilege granted poets. Since antiquity, he says, poets have used "figures and rhetorical effects to speak of inanimate things as though they had sense and reason." Love is a figure of speech.

By means of personification the poet builds a bridge between the invisible and the visible, the idea and the thing, the abstraction and the object. Love, envy, and wrath are passions that through the workings of language are transformed into persons, persons not of flesh and blood but imaginary. Personification is a moment in the process of allegory. The various personifications—Love, Envy, Chastity, Justice, Wrath, Temperance—speak among themselves as men and women do. Like men and women, they unite and separate, wage war on each other, and make peace. There is a difference, however: no matter what form they take, allegorical figures are not really forms but signs. The essence of the triangle is its form, which can be reduced to a geometrical and mathematical proportion. The triangle we see painted in a medieval church, however, is no longer a form: it is the sign of divinity. In allegory, the distance between being and meaning disappears: the sign devours the being. Each element of an allegory—face and body, gesture and dress—is an attribute, and each attribute is a sign. But allegory hides from us the very thing it presents to us. It is not a presence, though it assumes a corporeal form. It is a thing apprehended not with the eyes and all at once, but slowly and only with the mind. To see an allegory is to interpret it. We contemplate the forms of the world; we decipher allegories.

The intellectual nature of allegory is manifested also in the poet's attitude toward his work. Unlike the Romantic poet, possessed by inspiration, the allegorical poet is *completely aware* of what he is saying. Dante declares, simply and forthrightly: "It is most embarrassing for a poetaster, who cloaks his ideas with figures or with the colors of rhetoric, not to be able, when asked, to uncloak them, so that one can see their true meaning." Thus allegories, though they are presented as images, are really scriptures. Like Holy Scripture, the model of all scriptures, allegories conceal a plurality of meaning. In *Il convivio (The Banquet)* (II, 1), Dante calls his poems *scritture* and lists the four kinds of meaning that can be extracted from them: the literal, the allegorical ("the truth hidden by a beautiful lie"), the moral, and the anagogical or supernatural. The body of his allegory is quadruple—and ungraspable. Each meaning leads to another, higher one, and the last confronts us with that which cannot be expressed and lies beyond the realm of sense.

In the intelligent and learned book that C. S. Lewis has devoted to this subject *(The Allegory of Love),* he cautions us against a common confusion: reading a medieval allegory as though it were a symbol.* Allegory and symbol are brothers; both are manifestations of analogical thought, both postulate a secret relationship between the world of ideas and the world of things. But Lewis introduces a fundamental distinction: "This fundamental equivalence between the immaterial and the material may be used by the mind in two ways. . . . You can start with an immaterial fact, such as the passions you actually experience, and then can invent *visibilia* to express them. . . . We feel anger and imagine a person called Wrath with a torch. . . . This is allegory." On the other hand, we can also see our passions as a copy or reflection of an immaterial world. This was Plato's idea, and it is implicit—although seldom conscious—in all symbolism. Seeing the archetype through the copy, glimpsing in this world the world beyond, is what Lewis calls symbolism or sacramentalism. For the Symbolist, the reality we see is not entirely real; it is a symbol of the other reality, the true one. The idea, the essence.

Allegory was the favorite form of medieval poets, and we owe to it, among other works, *Le Roman de la rose.* However, despite the fact that Dante saw his poem as an allegory, the *Divine Comedy* is—fortunately—something else

---

*I confess that I myself am guilty of this confusion in the pages that, more than thirty years ago, I dedicated to Dante and the *Vita nuova* ("La inspiración," in *El arco y la lira*).

besides, and above all something irreducible to the obsessive, arid geometry of the genre. The decline of allegory begins in the Renaissance. The fantastic epic poem appears, in which the heroes and the circumstances are completely fictitious. The masterpiece of this new genre is Ariosto's *Orlando furioso,* a poem that few people read today, in spite of the fact that, with its vivacity, swift pace, and mixture of lofty poetry and humor, preposterousness and common sense, it is an extraordinarily modern book—a book that is alive. With the Italian burlesque epic—Boiardo and Ariosto—the hold of allegory is broken and the path is cleared to the novel and Cervantes. In the novel, a principle is at work that is the diametrical opposite of that of the allegorical poem: irony. Allegory revealed the correspondence between this world and the world beyond; the novel emphasizes the distance between the real and the imaginary.* The other great extensive poem of the Renaissance is also Italian: Tasso's *Gerusalemme liberata.* Less fast-paced and heterogeneous than the *Orlando,* it is graver and nobler. The humor evaporates and is transformed into the iridescent mist of melancholy.

Neither Italian epic poetry, though it is one of the most

---

*I have dealt with the subject of the contradictory relationship between analogy and irony in *El arco y la lira* (in the chapter "Ambigüedad de la novela"); in *El signo y el garabato* ("La nueva analogía"; Mexico City, 1973); and in *Los hijos del limo* ("Analogía e ironía").

sublime European literary creations, nor the other great poems of the Renaissance and the Baroque era—*Os Lusiadas, The Faerie Queene, Paradise Lost*—have exerted an influence on modern poetry. But the Romantics, Milton in particular, read them with fervor. The Romantics venerated their personal images, found in them emblems of the fate of the poet. Milton is blind and rebellious, Tasso love-smitten, mad, and persecuted. The indifference of modern readers toward the Renaissance and Baroque epics may come from the fact that these poems are the culmination of Greco-Latin and Renaissance humanism, whereas the Modern Age is the product of the breakdown of those aesthetic canons. This is a pity. Spenser's *Mutabilitie Cantos,* for instance, deserve to be read not with the eyes of literary archaeology but with those of today's poetry. They are modern despite the oldness of their language, modern because of their subject—the dialogue between mutation and identity, between change and continuity—and because of the vitality of their phrasing, images, and expression. Maximum abstraction put in particular and concrete terms. Nature, mother of all creatures, is "ever young yet full of eld, / Still moving, yet unmoved from her sted, / Unseen of any, yet of all beheld." Camoëns is less inclined to paradoxes and philosophies, but his language is no less concrete than Spenser's, and his narrative line is simpler. Economy of action and sumptuous digressions. Although Camoëns is remote from us, certain of his passages have not lost their

spellbinding power—the description, for instance, of
Malabar and its people, or the appearance of the giant
Adamastor transformed into the Cape of Good Hope
(which, with greater realism, the poet calls Cape of
Storms), or the delightful episode of the Isle of Love.

T. S. Eliot reproached Milton for his Latin expressions
and his eloquence—a surprising criticism, since it was tan-
tamount to reproaching him for what Eliot himself ex-
tolled: Europeanism. Inconsistency? Perhaps, rather, two
opposed visions of Europe. For Eliot, the European tradi-
tion could be summed up in two names: Rome and
Dante—that is, the medieval Christian order. For Milton,
Europe was above all the Greco-Roman past, the Renais-
sance humanities, reformed Christianity, and the new sci-
ence. During his travels in Italy, Milton visited Galileo,
who was living in seclusion. Milton's Europe is the Europe
that divided Eliot's Europe. The misunderstanding be-
tween Milton's generation and Eliot's is the same as that
which separates Michelangelo from painters such as Matisse
and Picasso. Milton was born forty years after the death of
Michelangelo, but there is a resemblance between them;
they are heroic personifications of the conflict between
Christianity and the ideal beauty of pagan humanism. In
the works of both artists, the Renaissance archetype of
humanity and nature triumphs: naturalistic idealism. The
figures they created possessed the more-than-human pro-
portions of the heroes of antiquity, and yet they were also

endowed with a dynamism absent in classical models and in the works of the painters and poets of the early Renaissance. The dynamism of Michelangelo and Milton is tragic, because it is a vision of the fall of the hero into endless space. By that I mean it is a version, at once Christian and Olympian, of the mystery of original sin.

Milton's Satan plunges interminably, and what is more terrible still, as he falls into the endless void, he falls into himself. Modernity begins with the discovery of this double infinite: the cosmic and the psychic. Humanity soon felt that it literally lacked ground to stand on. The new science had opened space, and through that cleft the human eye saw something resistant to thought: the infinite. Thus did modernity, newborn in poetry and art, discover a new vertigo. Dante's world was finite, hence he was able to trace the geography of hell, purgatory, and paradise. A limited world, but eternal: human beings were destined to live for all the centuries to come, and following the Last Judgment to experience no change whatsoever. Eternity does away with time and succession: what we are, we will be forever. This is the radical difference between the medieval and the modern world. The medieval Christian lived in a finite space and was destined for the eternity either of the blessed or of the damned; but we live in an infinite universe and are destined to disappear forever. Our condition is tragic in a sense that neither the pagans of antiquity nor the Christians of the Middle Ages suspected.

None of the Spanish epics of the sixteenth and seventeenth centuries is comparable to those I have mentioned. Lope de Vega, imitating Ariosto, wrote *La hermosura de Angélica,* and a few years later followed Tasso with his *Jerusalén conquistada.* Poems that deserved oblivion. Lope also wrote *Gatomaquia,* a burlesque epic that recounts the battles and love bouts of cats on the rooftops of Madrid. His cats are too human and his humans too stereotyped. And Alonso de Ercilla? A good many years ago Neruda, who was preparing to write his *Canto general,* insisted that I read the passages of Ercilla he admired. A reading at once boring and moving. Ercilla's style is like the trot of a cavalry squadron across a plain. But its monotony has its compensations: sobriety, realism, and a certain virile nobility. The lofty praise of the enemy, the cacique Caupolicán, is a lesson in poetic morality, especially in our own base era, which is in the habit of dishonoring the vanquished.

The fables that abounded in those centuries could be regarded as extensive poems, except that by their very nature they are episodes taken from the great book of mythology. Almost all of them were inspired by Ovid's *Metamorphoses.* The most famous, the *Fábula de Polifemo y Galatea,* is one of the most perfect poems in the European corpus—but is it an extensive poem? It has 504 verses—a long work to us, but not to readers of its day. Nor is *Soledades,* I think, an extensive poem. What is distinctive about the latter is not simply the number of lines but the development: the divisions between the various parts, and the relationships and articulations between them. An extensive poem must satisfy a twofold requirement: variety within unity and the combination of repetition and surprise. In *Soledades* I find not a development but an accumulation—sometimes dazzling, sometimes tedious and prolix—of fragments, details. I have been wanting to say this for some time and now finally dare to do so: *Soledades* is a sublime and pointless piece of marquetry. It has no action, no story, and is infested with long-winded amplifications and circumlocutions. The continual digressions are magic at times—it is like strolling through an enchanted garden—but eventually the marvels, the fascinating visions and meaningless riddles, become wearisome. Is it possible, really, to read *Soledades* with enthusiasm? Enthusiasm, divine frenzy, is the hallmark of poetry.

Composition is nonexistent in *Soledades*—composition in the sense in which the *Aeneid* and the *Divine Comedy,* the *Coplas a la muerte del maestro de Santiago* and *The Prelude,* the *Song of Myself* and *Un coup de dés* are *composed* works, whatever their genre. The *Polifemo,* which to me is Góngora's best poem, is more successfully conceived, perhaps because in this case the Cordovan poet faithfully followed Ovid. The action is as condensed and swift-moving as with the Latin poet, but Góngora's originality lies in the language, which is prodigious, and in his paradisiacal vision of the natural world. His characters impress us by their superhuman dimensions. His Polyphemus does not make us laugh, as does the one concocted by Theocritus, nor does he move us like the one we owe to Ovid: he astounds us. The same can be said of Acis and her unfortunate end, or of the beautiful Galatea and her passion: they cause us to marvel without winning, as do most heroes and heroines of literature, our sentimental or emotional complicity. They are not persons, not characters; they are images. Góngora's world is not the theater of human passions or the theater of the battles and loves of the gods; it is an aesthetic world, and its creatures, spun from words, are reflections, shadows, glimmers, illusions, adorable and ephemeral. What remains when the book is closed? A nature transfigured into language. Beauty.

Góngora's influence has been immense. He enriched our lexicon and taught us to see and to combine what we see in ways unusual and sensual; but he did not give us a vision of man or of this world and the worlds beyond. He did not teach us to *compose,* in the most immediate meaning of the word: to form a whole with different things. He was widely imitated, yet that influence produced no major work, save Sor Juana Inés de la Cruz's *Primero sueño.* The poem by the Mexican poetess is Gongorist, but at the same time it is the negation of Góngora and his aesthetic: a vision of the human spirit lost in the vastness of the universe. *Primero sueño* is a truly extensive poem, with a beginning, a complex development, and a sudden, unexpected end.

There is nothing in the poetry of our sixteenth and seventeenth centuries that resembles it. In the Spanish poetry of that time, it is a solitary obelisk. A poem of the act of knowing and of the limits of knowledge. One must go to Mallarmé's *Un coup de dés,* and to its descendants in our own century, to find similar visions and obsessions.

Although in more than one way we are the heirs of the eighteenth century, and its followers (not always faithful, having forgotten its tolerance and good manners), it is more distant poetically than the sixteenth or seventeenth century. In the eighteenth century, modernity came into being definitively, but modern poetry did not. The qualities of the extensive poems of that century were the opposite of the ones we love in the poems of the Romantics and the Symbolists. Pope's *Essay on Man,* for example, is a genuine essay—lucid, ingenious, elegant, and meticulously composed; yet I wonder whether, despite the admirable versification, it could not just as well have been written in prose. Milton's eloquence, on the other hand, sings to us, and his long and complex periods confuse us; and just as we are about to close the volume, a sudden spiritual perspective opens up before our eyes and holds us spellbound. It is as if the drop curtain of reality were torn apart and we could see *the other side.* Blake said that Milton, being a true poet, was on the devil's side without knowing it. Since then, Satan has been transformed into a figure who participates in the altruistic heroism of Prometheus, the daring of Icarus, and the love of freedom. Satan: subversion and irony, fall and melancholy. And the promise of redemption. The fallen prince—Lucifer, the morning star, the torchbearer who rends the darkness—fascinated the Romantics and their successors. In Victor Hugo's *La fin de Satan,* the rebellious angel sheds a feather in his infinite fall. Touched by God's eye, the feather turns into the angel Liberty.

Romanticism profoundly altered the extensive poem, its architecture and its subjects as well as its foundations. Romanticism was an innovation no less profound than that of allegory. In the first place, it introduced a subjective element as the subject of the poem: the *I* of the poet, his very person. In the second place, it made of the song the story itself. By that I mean the story of the song was the song; the subject of the poem was poetry itself. Or, as the aphoristic Machado puts it: a story is *sung,* a melody is *told.* To tell is simultaneously to relate and put in verse: I recount that the story becomes a song, and I sing that the song tells the story. The Romantic poem has as its subject the song, the singer: the poem, the poet. In the *Divine Comedy,* the hero is not a demigod but a sinner: the Florentine poet Dante Alighieri, who is a real person but at the same time an allegory of fallen man. The subject of Byron's *Don Juan* is not the libertine of the Sevillian legend but the poet himself. Don Juan is not an allegory of Byron; he is a symbolic mask, a persona. Byron is both Byron and the reflection that transcends him: the free, rebel poet. The earthly reflection, the spiritual and corporeal copy of an archetype: Satan, the angel of freedom.

The symbol operates in the opposite direction of allegory. Blake writes an epic-symbolic poem that has Milton as a figure in it, but Blake's Milton is actually Blake himself, who in turn is the human manifestation of the poetic imagination. According to Blake, imagination has the mission to convert, through the poet, "the sons of Memory" (Greco-Roman poetry) into "the sons of inspiration" (the poetry of the new era). Blake's Milton, the embodiment of "eternal energy" (Satan), is not an allegory: he is the *symbol* of the new poet. The new poetry aims at putting an end to the imitation of "the perverted writings of Virgil, Ovid and the other pagans, slaves of the sword." In Blake's Milton, the poem of the poet and the poem of poetry are conjoined.

It is not difficult to find these two notes, invariably in the symbolic mode, in almost all the great Romantic poems: Hölderlin's *Hyperion,* Shelley's *Adonais,* Coleridge's *The Rime of the Ancient Mariner.* In *The Prelude,* the two elements appear directly and explicitly. Wordsworth tells us of the making of the poet Wordsworth, from his visionary infancy to maturity. But it is not a biography, though real-life episodes are not omitted. The true hero of *The Prelude* is the poetic imagination: how it is born in a child; how it fades and is about to be lost; and how, through the contemplation of nature and human society, the mature poet brings it back to life. It is a poem animated by a double movement: the passage to maturity is also a return to childhood. The subject of the poem is psychological, philosophical, and above all poetic and religious: to regain the eyes of the child. The reclamation of innocent knowledge. The poem of the poet becomes one with the poem of the poem.

Symbolism took up these two great themes of Romantic poetry, the poetry of the poet and the poetry of the poem, and between these two poles, it laid bare—another Romantic heritage—the dialogue between irony and analogy. Between the awareness of time and the vision of universal correspondence. A dialogue that ends in discord, as in Baudelaire. Symbolist poetry introduced another change, this one truly radical: it applied to the extensive poem the aesthetics of the short poem. The Symbolist poem detests explanations: it does not tell or even say; it suggests. Its song borders on silence. One of the elements of the extensive poem was the continuity of its development, that is to say, the linear nature of the composition: episode followed episode, each linked to the one before and the one after, without break or rupture. The Symbolist poet destroys this continuity: he values the pause, the blank space. A Symbolist poem is an archipelago of fragments. The development is atomized. Unlike the fragments of the

Romantic poem, they are not connected by a verbal chain but by silences, affinities, colors. Succession is tacit, not explicit. Finally, metaphors and symbols abound in the Symbolist poem, while descriptions and narration are omitted. An encounter between the extensive and the intensive: the extensive poem becomes a sequence of intense moments.

The best example of the new poetics was *Un coup de dés,* a strange poem that has as its subject the act of writing a poem. But a poem never before attempted: an absolute poem. Not *a* poem on the poem but *the* poem on the poem. The subject of Sor Juana Inés de la Cruz—the poem of the act of knowing—reappears, carried to an extreme. The reply was equally negative: *the* poem on the poem was *a* poem on the poem. There is no other poem except the one I am now writing in a language destined to disappear. Hence the poem of the poem of Hölderlin and the other Romantics culminates in its criticism and negation: we are condemned to write the same poem, and each version of this universal poem is particular and relative. The emotion with which Mallarmé discovered Hegel's system of thought, in 1866, is a well-known fact. There is an undoubted affinity between the philosopher and the poet: both take as their point of departure the ultimate equation of being and nothing.*

---

*An idea that can also be found in the thought of India, particularly in the Buddhism of Nagarjuna.

According to Hegel, the dialectic is destined to mediate between the various modes of being until its full and final affirmation. This idea corresponds to Mallarmé's ambition to reduce chance (language) to an absolute number (the poem). Arriving at a position dramatically opposed to that of the arrogant Hegel—and in this regard Mallarmé's humility was wisdom as well—he ends up uttering little more than a "perhaps." The poetic dice box cannot rule out chance: there is no absolute number. If there were, it would be unknowable and inexpressible. Each poem, each number, is an instantaneous absolute. A lesson in sobriety and heroism. It was a return implicit in Kant, although Mallarmé may not have been aware of this. Kant, the founder of true modernity, was the first to warn us against the deliriums of the dialectic, which he rightfully called the "philosophy of illusion."

At the other extreme: Walt Whitman. To have an idea of his extraordinary modernity, it is necessary to recall the date of publication of *Song of Myself:* 1855. What was being written at that time in Europe and in America? Mallarmé's poem appeared nearly half a century later, in 1897. But more than a date separates the two poets: their works point to the contrary—though complementary—paths that the poetry of the twentieth century will follow. Whitman takes up the Romantic theme of the poet as the subject of the poem. At the same time he radically changes this tradition. He does not tell us the story of a legendary hero, behind whose physical form the poet conceals himself, as in Hölderlin's *Hyperion* or Byron's *Childe Harold*. Nor does he write a poetic biography in the manner of Wordsworth's *Prelude*. *Song of Myself* is not a poetic account but a poetic *expansion*. Whitman does not speak of the vicissitudes of his life or of his own self. The poet sings of an *I* that is a *you* and a *he* and a *we*. He is one among many, and a unique being; a wanderer on foot, and a cosmos. The time of the song is also unprecedented, for it is neither a mythical past nor an atemporal present. It is a closed present, 1855, and a present that has no dates at all: the here and now that comes and goes every day, ever since human beings became human. Whitman regains the archetypal nature of time not by way of a legendary past but through immersion in the present moment. What is happening right now is happening always.

The form of the poem, too, is in direct contrast to Mallarmé's. Both eschew rhyme, but while Mallarmé's rhythm is primordially visual—the disposition of the lines on the pages, the blank spaces, and the different letters—Whitman's is oral: something we do not see but hear. A return to the origin of poetry: the spoken word. Mallarmé extols reticence, silence, blanks; his language comes from writing and is exquisite. Whitman's language is spoken, and its excesses are not from preciosity but from preachiness and gesticulation. In his enthusiasm, the poet wants to say everything. He both loses and gains by indulging in interminable enumeration with a delight that is at once infantile and cosmic; he ranges from secret sharing to expostulation to prophecy. As he exalts the *I,* he exalts the *we.* His democracy is libertarian, egalitarian, and cosmic. A poem on the reconciliation of inimical powers: the body and the soul, the present and the past, the *I* and the *you,* the white and the black, the man and the woman, the high and the low. *Song of Myself* ends as the song of the foundation of a free community, a fraternity among men and between men and things, be they stars or mice, tigers or locomotives, trees or sonnets. Mallarmé: the song of the solitary poet in the face of the universe. Whitman: the founding song of the free community of equals. With these two poets, one modernity ends—Romantic poetry, Symbolism—and another begins: our own.

MEXICO CITY, 1976

Breach and Convergence

You say I am repeating
Something I have said before.
I shall say it again.
Shall I say it again?
— T. S. Eliot

MODERNITY AND ROMANTICISM

The subject I propose to explore is poetry and modernity, whose relation to each other is far from clear. The poetry of the last years of this century is the heir of the poetic movements of modernity, from Romanticism to today's avant-gardes, but it is also a repudiation of them. Nor is it obvious what is meant by the word *modernity*. The first difficulty we encounter is the elusive and ever-changing

---

This text was read in a summer course at the Universidad Menéndez Pelayo (Santander) in 1986 and later, in 1989, at the Collège de France and the University of Utah (Tanner Lectures).

nature of the word itself. What is "modern" is inherently transitory; "contemporary" is a quality that vanishes the moment we name it. There are as many modernities and antiquities as there are eras and societies: the Aztecs were moderns compared to the Olmecs, as was Alexander compared to Amenhotep IV. The "modernist" poetry of Rubén Darío was an antique for the Ultraists, and Futurism now strikes us as more a relic than an aesthetic. The Modern Age will soon be tomorrow's antiquity. But for the moment we must resign ourselves and accept the fact that we live in the Modern Age, though we know that the label is both ambivalent and provisional.

What do we mean by this word *modernity*? When did it begin? Some believe it began with the Renaissance, the Reformation, and the discovery of America; others claim it originated with the birth of the nation-states and the institution of banking, the rise of mercantile capitalism and the emergence of the bourgeoisie; and others emphasize the scientific and philosophical revolutions of the seventeenth century, without which we would have neither technology nor industry. Each of these opinions has something to recommend it. By itself, each is only partially correct; together, they form a coherent explanation. For that reason, perhaps, most cultural historians tend to favor the eighteenth century: not only did it inherit these changes and innovations, but it was also consciously aware of many of the characteristics that would one day be our own. Was that age a prefiguration, then, of the age we live in today? Yes and no. It would be more accurate to say that ours has been the age of the distortion of the ideas and visions of that great century.

Modernity began as a critique of religion, philosophy, morality, law, history, economics, and politics. Criticism was its most distinctive feature, its hallmark. Everything the Modern Age represents has been the work of criticism, in the sense of a method of investigation, creation, and action. The key concepts of the Modern Age—progress, evolution, revolution, freedom, democracy, science, technology—had their origin in criticism. In the eighteenth century, reason turned to the criticism of the world and of itself, thereby radically transforming classical rationalism and its timeless geometries. A criticism of itself: reason renounced the grandiose constructions that made it synonymous with Being, Good, or Truth; it ceased to be the Mansion of the Idea and became instead a path, a means of exploration. A criticism of metaphysics, and of its truths impermeable to change: Hume and Kant. A criticism of the world, of the past and present; a criticism of certainties and traditional values; a criticism of institutions and beliefs, of the Throne and the Altar; a criticism of mores, passions, sensibility, and sexuality: Rousseau, Diderot, Choderlos de Laclos, Sade. And the historical criticism of Gibbon and Montesquieu: The discovery of the *other* in the Chinese, the Persian, the American Indian. The changes of perspective in astronomy, geography, physics, biology. In the end, a criticism embodied in historical events: the American Revolution, the French Revolution, the independence movement of the Spanish and Portuguese colonies. (For reasons I have discussed in other writings, the revolution for independence in Spanish and Portuguese America failed both politically and socially. Our modernity is incomplete—or, more precisely, it is a historical hybrid.)

It is no accident that these great revolutions, the roots of modern history, were inspired by eighteenth-century thought. It was an age that produced an abundance of utopias and projects for social reform. It has been said that these utopias are the least auspicious aspect of the eighteenth century's legacy. Yet we can neither ignore nor condemn them: though many horrors have been committed in their name, we also owe to them nearly all the humanitarian acts and dreams of the Modern Age. The utopias of the eighteenth century were the great ferment that set in motion the history of the next two centuries. Utopia is the reverse side of criticism, and only a critical age can be the inventor of such dreams. The empty spaces left by the demolitions of the critical spirit are almost always filled by utopian constructions. Utopias are the dreams of reason—dreams that can turn, active, into revolutions and reforms. The importance of utopias is another characteristic of the Modern Age. Each age may be identified by its vision of time, and in ours the continual presence of revolutionary utopias bears witness to the privileged place we give the future. The past was no better than the present is; perfection lies not behind us, but ahead of us. It is not a forsaken paradise, but a territory we must one day colonize, a city we must one day build.

Christianity replaced the old Greco-Roman cyclical vision of time with a time that was linear, successive, and irreversible, one that had a beginning and an end, proceeding from the Fall of Adam and Eve to the Last Judgment. Opposed to this mortal and historical time was another time, supernatural, invulnerable to death and change: Eternity. The only truly decisive moment of earthly history, therefore, was the Redemption. The descent and sacrifice of Christ represents the intersection of temporality with Eternity, of the successive, mortal time of man with the time of the beyond, which, forever identical to itself, neither changes nor passes. The Modern Age began with the criticism of Christian Eternity and, accompanying it, the appearance of another kind of time. On the one hand the finite time of Christianity, with its beginning and end, became the nearly infinite time of the evolution of nature and history, a time ever open to the future. On the other, modernity devalued Eternity: perfection was transported to a future that lay not in the next world but in this one. In Hegel's famous image, the rose of reason is crucified in the present. History, he said, is a Calvary, a transformation of the Christian mystery into historical action. The road to the Absolute travels by means of time; it *is* time. Change and revolution are the embodiments of the human march toward the future and its paradises.

The relation between Romanticism and modernity was at once filial and rent with controversy. Romanticism was the child of the Age of Criticism, and change was responsible for its birth and was its sign of identity. Change not only in the realm of arts and letters, but also in imagination, sensibility, taste, and ideas. Romanticism was an ethic, an eroticism, a politics, a way of dressing, a way of living and dying. A rebellious child, Romanticism was a criticism of rational criticism. To historical time it preferred the time of origins, before history; to the utopian future it preferred the immediate present of the passions, love, and the flesh. Romanticism was the great negation of modernity as it had been conceived in the eighteenth century by critical, utopian, and revolutionary reason—but it was a negation that remained within modernity. Only the Age of Criticism could have produced such a total negation.

Romanticism coexisted with modernity, again and again merging with it only in order to transgress against it. These transgressions assumed many forms but manifested themselves in only two modes: analogy and irony. By analogy I mean "the vision of the universe as a system of correspondences and the vision of language as a double of the universe."* This is a very old idea, re-elaborated and transmitted by Renaissance Neoplatonism through various Hermetic traditions of the sixteenth and seventeenth centuries. After having nourished the philosophical and libertine sects of the eighteenth century, it was taken up by the Romantics and their followers and passed on to our own era. It is the central, yet underground, tradition of modern poetry, from the first Romantics to Yeats, Rilke, and the Surrealists. As this vision of universal correspondence appeared, its enemy twin simultaneously appeared: irony. Irony was the tear in the fabric of analogies, the interruption in the current of the correspondences. If analogy may be thought of as a fan which, when unfolded, reveals the resemblances between *this* and *that,* microcosm and macrocosm, stars, humans, and worms, then irony rips this fan to pieces. Irony is the dissonance that disrupts the concert and turns it into cacophony. Irony has many names: the anomaly, the exception, the *bizarre,* as Baudelaire called it. In a word, it is that catastrophic accident: death.

Analogy has a definite place, plays an integral role, in myth: its essence is rhythm, the cyclical time of appearances and disappearances, deaths and resurrections. Irony is the incursion of criticism into the kingdom of imagination and sensibility: Its time is linear, leading to death—the death both of humans and of gods. (The theme of the death of

---

*See *Los hijos del limo.*

God appears in the modern consciousness at the same time
as the first texts of the Romantics.)* A mutual transgres-
sion: analogy replaces the linear time of history and the
canonization of the utopian future with the cyclical time of
myth; irony, in turn, shreds mythical time in order to
affirm the fall into accident, the plurality of gods and myths,
the death of God and of his creatures. The twin ambiguities
of Romantic poetry. First, it was revolutionary, yet it came
into being not with but in spite of the revolutions of the
century. Second, its religiosity flew in the face of all Chris-
tian denominations. The history of modern poetry, from
Romanticism to Symbolism, is the history of the various
manifestations of the two principles that have constituted it
since its birth: analogy and irony.

MODERNITY AND THE AVANT-GARDE

The nineteenth century may be seen as the apogee of
modernity. The ideas that were born of criticism, and that
had a polemical value, in the eighteenth century—democ-
racy; the separation of Church and State, the end of royal
privileges; freedom of beliefs, opinions, and association—
became, in the nineteenth, the principles shared by nearly
all the European nations and the United States. The West
expanded, extended its boundaries, and asserted its hegem-

---

*Jean Paul (Richter). See also *Los hijos del limo,* chapter 3.

ony. But at the end of the last century, a deep malaise began
to be felt in the great centers of our civilization, a malaise
that affected social, political, and economic systems as well
as systems of beliefs and values. We may name the cycle
that includes the birth, apogee, and crisis of modernity the
Modern Age. The last stage, that of crisis, is the Contem-
porary Era, but its duration—it has lasted nearly a cen-
tury—leads me to doubt that the term is appropriate. The
words that invariably appear when one addresses this
topic—decadence, decline, twilight—are equally unsuit-
able. And *crisis* has been weakened from overuse. But
whatever name we give it, the period that began at the start
of this century is distinguishable from the others by its
uncertainty as regards the values and ideas that constituted
the basis of modernity. The first signs of this universal crisis
appeared at the end of the last century; by 1910, they were
brutally clear. I need not describe them. For a long time
now, they have been the favorite topic of sociologists,
astrologers, clergymen, economists, prophets, psychoana-
lysts, journalists, and the other faith healers of the ills of
our society.

The birth of the Modern Age also brought the blos-
soming of that great upheaval and great aberration: na-
tionalism. Transformed into the religion of the State,
nationalism acquired, in the last century, a tremendous
ferocity. Meanwhile, the reactionary criticism of bourgeois
democracy—rationalism, cosmopolitanism, skepticism, he-

donism—allied itself with a nostalgia for precapitalist socie-
ties and their "idyllic relations," as Marx ironically put it.
In these sermons against the sins of progress there were
echoes of the ancient Christian horror of Satan, that skepti-
cal, intelligent Mammon, lover of industry, pleasure, and
the arts. At the other end of the political spectrum, but with
equal passion, the revolutionaries—above all, the anar-
chists—denounced the oppressive nature of the State and
of social institutions: the family, property, the law. In the
first phase of the crisis, Marxist socialism was critical but
not subversive; the Second International did much to im-
prove the lot of workers, but it maintained its ties to the
established institutions of the industrial nations.

In the second decade of the twentieth century, the
crisis of social institutions became a crisis of international
politics, which led to the explosive outbreak of the First
World War. The revolutions that followed changed the
face of the planet. Marxism—or more precisely its authori-
tarian version, Leninism—became a world power. In the
third decade, under various names and with contradictory
ideologies, it embodied a new historical reality: the bureau-
cratic totalitarian State. This process has continued every-
where throughout the remainder of the century. Even the
countries that preserve a democratic system have copied
the model of bureaucratic domination, whether in the
huge capitalistic consortia, the workers' unions, or the
technocratic states. Few people suspected, at the beginning

of this century, that the benevolent aspirations of the day, libertarian and revolutionary, would degenerate, fifty years later, into a new absolutism.

This crisis of public life was also a crisis of conscience. A criticism of the family and of male domination, a criticism of sexual morality, a criticism of the schools, of churches, of beliefs and values. Despite the immense technological gains, there began to be doubts about progress, the great ruling principle of the West and its principal intellectual myth. The spiritual mood that prevailed in the first half of the century, with its violent oscillations between passivity and violence, between radical skepticism and faith in instinct, between extreme intellectualism and the cult of blood sacrifice, has been described many times, and the picture need not be repeated here. I would merely like to point out that these oscillations coincided with certain fundamental discoveries in the sciences, discoveries which, in similar fashion, called into question the hallowed certainties. Non-Euclidian geometry, quantum theory, relativity, the fourth dimension. To these advances there have been added, more recently, those of molecular biology and genetics. If age-old mind evaporated, turned into nothing more than a chemical reaction, age-old matter equally lost its mass, becoming pure energy in time-space, a reality that endlessly expands and endlessly falls back into itself. If matter has broken down into atoms and particles of particles, what can we say of consciousness? Consciousness has ceased to be the cornerstone of the individual. For some, it has become a theater of war for new entities—entities perhaps no less illusory than those of Renaissance psychology: the subconscious, the id, the libido, the superego. For others, thought and emotion are now no more than the product of physiological and chemical combinations. The family is transformed into a nursery for fantasies, and the crime of Oedipus takes on the universal dignity previously attributed to original sin: an essential mark of the human species, a feature distinguishing it from all the other species.

Art and literature are representations of reality. Representations that are, I need hardly add, also inventions: imaginary. But reality itself, in this century, acquired the attributes of the imaginary; it became threatening, contemptible, inconsistent, fantastic. A chair ceased to be the chair that we saw; it was now a construct of invisible forces, atoms, particles. Not only did the new physics undermine the solidity of material objects, but non-Euclidian geometries opened up the possibility of other spaces, spaces with entirely different properties. A new concept was born, the subject of endless lucubrations by writers and painters and the central myth of the first avant-garde: time-space. Only later, in the next generation—that of the Surrealists—did psychoanalysis influence poets and painters. Since then, the vision of the *I* and of the self has undergone profound changes, and with it the language of artists seeking to express the discontinuities and intermittences of consciousness and the senses.

Symbolism had allied itself with an esoteric language. A cult of the mystery of the universe; a cult of the poet as high priest of a secret religion. The new poets countered that language with irony and prosaicism. Symbolism had exalted chiaroscuro; it was an indoor art that took subtle shadings as its supreme value. The new art went out into the streets: a poetry of sharp contrasts and brutal oppositions. Symbolism had expressed a nostalgia for the beyond, a beyond located in an impossible past or a no less impossible *nowhere*. The new poetry celebrated the moment, the present: what the eyes see, what the hands touch. Baudelaire's city had been an urban night scene in which the gaslights and their reflections—as ambiguous as human consciousness—lit the woundlike streets and their parade of prostitution, crime, and solitary despair. But the city of the modern poets was a city of crowds, brightly lit advertisements, streetcars, and automobiles, a city that every night transformed itself into an electric garden. But this modern city was no less terrible than Baudelaire's: "Now you walk in pairs alone among the crowd / and herds of bellowing buses hemming you in / the anguish of love grips you by the throat."*

The Romantic hero was an adventurer, a pirate, a poet

---

*Guillaume Apollinaire, "Zone," 1912.

turned freedom fighter, or a solitary figure on the bank of a deserted lake, lost in sublime meditation. Baudelaire's hero was an angel fallen into the city: he dressed in black, his elegant, threadbare suit stained with wine, oil, and mud. Apollinaire's hero is an urban vagabond, almost a bum, ridiculous and pathetic, lost in the crowd. It is the figure later embodied in Charlie Chaplin, in Mayakovski's *Cloud in Trousers,* in Pessoa's *Tobacco Shop.* A poor devil endowed with occult powers, a clown and magus. Such characters were new, but at the same time they were direct descendants of Romanticism.

Although the human adventure—its passions, madnesses, moments of illumination—continued to unfold in the new poetry, the speakers changed. The ancient natural world had disappeared and along with it its forests, valleys, oceans, and mountains inhabited by monsters, gods, demons, and other fabulous beings. In its place appeared the abstract city and, among the old monuments and venerable public squares, the terrible newness of machines. A change of reality, a change of mythology. In the past, men spoke with the universe, or thought they did: if it did not answer, it was at least their mirror. In the twentieth century, the mythical speaker and the mysterious voices have vanished. Each man is alone in the enormous city, sharing his solitude with solitary millions. The hero of the new poetry is a loner in a crowd of loners. He is Joyce's H.C.E. (Here Comes Everybody). We discovered that we were alone in the universe—alone with our machines. Milton's industrious devils must have rubbed their hands in glee. It was the beginning of the great solipsism.

The ancients worshiped the horse and the sailing ship; the new age worshiped the train and the ocean liner. The poem of Whitman's that most influenced his followers was probably the one dedicated to a locomotive. Valéry Larbaud wrote a memorable ode to the Orient Express, "the train of millionaires." Blaise Cendrars's equally memorable "Prose of the Trans-Siberian" is the first marriage of poetry and film. The Futurists hymned the automobile, and later there were countless poems devoted to the airplane, the submarine, and other modern vehicles. But none of these dogged texts can compare with Whitman's original poem. Transatlantic liners also fired the imagination. Alvaro de Campos—the pseudonymous de Campos was neither an allegory nor a symbol of Fernando Pessoa, but his double and his enemy—wrote "Oda marítima" not only on the docks of Lisbon, but also in Liverpool, Singapore, Yokohama, Harbin. The ocean liner was associated, in the poetry of this period, more with Asia than the Americas. The first act of Claudel's *Partage de midi* takes place on a steamer endlessly plying the Indian Ocean. The poetry of the sea was a poetry of the beyond: not only unknown seas and lands, but also other civilizations: Kipling's India, Conrad's Africa and Southeast Asia, the Far East of Claudel and Saint-John Perse.

The presence of the landscapes and the artistic forms of the Orient, Africa, and pre-Columbian America is a major feature of the poetry and art of those years. Poets adopted the haiku, and the Noh theater influenced Yeats and other playwrights. Ezra Pound translated Chinese poetry. In short, the first third of the twentieth century was the culmination of a long process of discovery of *other* civilizations and their various visions of reality and humanity. This process, begun in the sixteenth century with the exploration of the American continent, resulted in our time in the adoption of artistic forms that were not only different from but contrary to the mainstream tradition of the West. A change so profound, it still affects us, and will affect the arts and the sensibilities of those who follow us. It was the natural result, the extreme consequence, of the aesthetic revolution that began with Romanticism; it was also the ultimate change, the change of changes, ending a tradition that had begun with the Renaissance. The models of that tradition were the works of Greco-Roman antiquity. By denying them, modern art broke the continuity of the West. Thus the change was both a self-denial and a metamorphosis. An end of idealized Nature, of perspective and the golden section, of representations intended to give the illusion of reality.

The decisive factor here was not the replacement of traditional canons—including their Romantic, Symbolist, and Impressionist variations—with foreign cultures and civilizations but, rather, the search for *other* forms of beauty. For this reason I spoke not only of self-denial but also of metamorphosis. The aesthetic change was no less far-reaching than the change in our view of reality wrought by science. Physics had shown that visible reality was dependent on a structure that was a relationship of forces in unstable equilibrium. Artists similarly attempted to dismantle the visibility of everyday objects, and the Cubists in particular conceived of a painting as a system of equations. There was a sort of Neoplatonism in this notion: the painter representing the structure—the archetype, the *idea*—of the coffeepot or the pipe. Hence the need to paint both the exterior and the interior of an object. The example of African masks, which contain both front and back on the same plane, was instructive. The Futurists for their part wanted to paint motion, something that photography does much better than painting. In that period, the chrono-photograph was popular: a series of consecutive instants of a figure in motion, a horse running, a woman walking rhythmically, a cyclist. The most notable example in painting is Marcel Duchamp's *Nude Descending a Staircase.*

All these experiments were influenced by the new techniques of reproducing reality. The major attraction, particularly for the poets, was photography in motion: the cinema. The great theoretician of montage, Sergei Eisenstein, notes in one of his essays that the absence of rules of syntax and punctuation marks in film had revealed to him the true nature of this art: juxtaposition and simultaneity. In other words, the breakup of the linear nature of narrative. Eisenstein discovered predecessors of the use of simultaneity in the art of the East: Japanese theater, Chinese ideography. Years later Jung, in his preface to an edition of the Chinese classic the *I Ching,* maintained that the principle that rules the hexagrams is not causality but confluence. Causality assumes that one thing follows another, that one event is the cause of another event. The *I Ching* depends on the simultaneous presence of a number of causes. Jung called this coincidence *synchronicity,* a conjunction of times that is also a conjunction of spaces. In short, in the second decade of the twentieth century there appeared in painting, poetry, and the novel an art of temporal and spatial conjunctions that both dissolved and juxtaposed the dichotomies of before and after, front and back, internal and external. This art had many names; the best of them, the most descriptive, was Simultaneism.

Painters advanced the notion that a painting should be a simultaneous presentation of the various facets of an object. A Cubist painting showed both the interior and exterior of the object, the front and back of reality, while a Futurist painting provided the before and after: a dog running, a trolley crossing a public square. Painting is a spatial art; the eye can see at the same time a number of representations and forms on a single surface. Sight is simultaneous. Juxtaposition results in a system of visual relations. The principle ruling this type of representation is *contiguity*: things next to each other are perceived simultaneously. In the temporal arts, such as music and poetry, things follow one after the other. Sound follows sound, word follows word. The ruling principle here is not contiguity but *succession*. Yet there is an essential difference between music and poetry. In music, synchrony is continual: counterpoint, harmony, the fugue. Poetry, however, is made of words—sounds that are meanings. Each sound must be heard clearly, so that the listener will understand its meaning. Harmony, the essence of music, in poetry produces only confusion. Poetry cannot be synchronous without going against its very nature and renouncing the great power of the word. And yet simultaneity is a powerful device present in the basic elements of the poem. Comparison, metaphor, rhythm, and rhyme are conjunctions and repetitions that obey the same laws as simultaneous presentation. This was the challenge that confronted poets around 1910: How to adapt spatial simultaneity to an art ruled by temporal *succession*?

In 1911, "Dramatism" made its appearance in Paris; it was later called "Simultaneism." Both the word and the concept had been used slightly earlier by the Futurists. The procedure was simplicity itself: different parts of the poem were read aloud at the same time. The Futurist solution was even more chaotic: "concerts" were given, in which the human voice, reduced to elements of pure sound ranging from shouts to whispers, was jumbled with such urban noises as the clatter of typewriters. Later, in Zurich during the war, the Dadaist Hugo Ball rediscovered the "speaking in tongues" of the early Christians, the Gnostics, and other religions. In Moscow and Saint Petersburg, at about the same time, the Russian Futurists exploited the possibilities of glossolalia, which they called "transrational language." But this reduction of language to mere rhythmical emissions, while it permitted juxtaposition and simultaneity, also reduced meaning to a minimum. It was an impoverishment, and almost always a mutilation.

Cubism, and above all the Orphism of Delaunay, inspired the first experiments by Cendrars and Apollinaire, with whom Simultaneism truly began. In the case of Cendrars especially, the influence of film techniques—montage, flashback—was decisive. The use of cinematographic devices shattered syntax and the linear, successive nature of traditional poetry. Apollinaire went even further: he almost totally omitted connectives and conjunctions—a procedure analogous to the elimination of perspective in painting—and applied the technique of collage, incorporating the text phrases, blocks of words, found at random. In this way he succeeded in creating a fusion of space and time on a single page. Unlike the paintings of the Cubists, Apollinaire's poems move. By this I mean that they not only have a beginning and an end but also *elapse*. Futurism had attempted to represent movement; the new poetry was movement itself. Other French poets followed Apollinaire in this direction—I am thinking especially of Pierre Reverdy.

Some years later, Pound and Eliot adopted Simultaneism. In adopting it, they transformed and extended it, creating a new form of the extensive poem and exploring territory untouched by the French poets: the spiritual and social history of the West. In Spanish, Simultaneism, with the exception of a short and perfect poem by José Juan Tablada, was not pursued until my generation. It is worth making a complaint here, a complaint I have made before: American critics, with the exception of Roger Shattuck, the poet Kenneth Rexroth, and a few others, never refer to the French origins of Simultaneism; they persist in repeating Pound's claim that his method of *presentation,* as he called it, grew out of his translations of Chinese poetry and his reading of Fenollosa. I have attempted on various occasions to correct this error, but because of the extraordinary influence of Anglo-American culture, the critics—and they include a goodly number in Latin America and even France—adhere to the canonical version. No one wants to see the *Cantos* and *The Waste Land* as a product of the Simultaneism introduced ten years earlier by Apollinaire and Cendrars. A product, of course, that was also a creation: not an imitation but a grafting, a new plant, one vaster, more complex, and more powerful than the original.

Simultaneism, sometimes called Poetic Cubism, was

yet another manifestation, often crude but nearly always effective, of the cardinal principle of Romantic and Symbolist poetry: analogy. A poem is a totality propelled—and impelled—by the complementary action of affinities and oppositions between its parts. A triumph of contiguity over succession. Or, more precisely, a fusion, spatial and temporal, of the two. Shortly thereafter, at the other extreme of avant-garde poetry—Surrealism—both analogy and humor reappeared in an even more overt, direct manner. All the great poetic, erotic, and metaphysical themes of Romanticism were taken up by the Surrealists and carried to their limits. The axis of the two great poetic movements of the first half of the twentieth century—Simultaneism and Surrealism—was the same as that of Romanticism: the vision of universal correspondence and the consciousness of a break, of death. The ambiguous relation of Romanticism to Western religious traditions and revolutionary political movements also reappeared in nearly all the great poets of our century. Since its birth, modern poetry has been simultaneously an affirmation and a negation of modernity.

THE POETRY OF CONVERGENCE

With a certain regularity, voices are raised to warn us that the end is near. It seems that modernity has nourished itself on the successive negations it engendered, from Chateaubriand to Nietzsche, from Nietzsche to Valéry. In the last twenty-five years, these voices full of calamity and catastrophe have greatly multiplied. They are not the anguished cry from a despairing loner or a small group of nonconformists, but now widespread, popular opinion, the voice of the collective spirit. The temper of this century is reminiscent, at times, of the terrors of the year 1000 or of the dark vision of the Aztecs, who lived under the threat of the cyclical end of the cosmos. Modernity was born when the future was proclaimed to be a promised land; today we are witnessing the decline of that idea. No one is sure of what awaits us, and many wonder if humanity will see the sun rise tomorrow. The future has been discredited in so many ways, it is impossible to list them all. The depletion of natural resources, the contamination of the planet, famine, the petrification of history by the universal restoration of totalitarian ideocracies, and atomic holocaust. Nuclear deterrence is keeping us from a Third World War, yes, but for how long? And even if we succeed in avoiding catastrophe, the very existence of atomic weapons explodes our idea of progress, whether it is the progress of gradual evolution or revolutionary leap. If the bomb has not yet destroyed the world, it has destroyed our idea of the world. Modernity is a fatal wound: the sun of progress has set on the horizon, and we have not yet seen the rise of a new star to guide us. We cannot tell whether we are living in a twilight or a dawn.

Modernity identified itself with change, conceived of criticism as the agent of change, and equated both to progress. For Marx, revolutionary insurrection was criticism in action. In the realm of literature and the arts, the aesthetic of modernity from Romanticism to our own time has been the aesthetic of change. The discovery of the arts of other civilizations—India and the Far East, Africa and Oceania, pre-Columbian America—has also been experienced as a break with the traditions of the West. Today we are witnessing the sunset of this aesthetic of change and rupture. The art and literature of the last years of this century have slowly lost their power of negation. For some time now their negation has been ritualized repetition, their rebellion a formula, their transgression a ceremony. It is not the end of art: it is the end of the *idea* of modern art.

Criticism, after a certain lag, finally noticed that in the past quarter of a century we have embarked upon another period of history and another art. There is a great deal of talk about the crisis of the avant-garde, and to denote our own period, the expression "postmodernist era" has been widely used. A label as ambivalent and contradictory as modernism itself. What comes after the modern cannot be anything but ultramodern: a modernity even more modern than yesterday's. People have never known the name of the age in which they live, and we are no exception to this rule. To call ourselves "postmodern" is merely a naive way of saying that we are extremely modern. And yet what has not been called into question is the linear concept of time and its identification with criticism, change, and progress—time opening into the future as a promised land. To call ourselves postmodern is to continue to be the prisoner of successive, linear, progressive time.

If the term *postmodern* is more a mask than a name, what can be said about the expression used by Anglo-American critics as a label for contemporary art: *postmodernism*? For these critics the word *modernism* designates the community of works, authors, and tendencies evoked by such names as Joyce, Pound, Eliot, William Carlos Williams, Hemingway, and others. Yet nearly everyone (except perhaps Anglo-American critics and reviewers) knows that in Spanish what we call *modernismo* is the first literary movement in Latin America and in Spain. Rubén Darío and Valle-Inclán, Juan Ramón Jiménez and Leopoldo Lugones, José Martí and Antonio Machado were all *modernistas*: with them our modern tradition begins, and without them our contemporary literature would not exist. The fact is that what the Anglo-Americans lump together under the term *modernism* was always known in France—and the rest of Europe, and Latin America—by a term that is equally vague: the avant-garde.* To ignore this, to use the word *modernism* to apply exclusively to a movement in the

---

*One example, from hundreds like it: Guillermo de la Torre's *Literaturas de vanguardia,* published in 1925.

English language that came thirty years later, is to show cultural arrogance, ethnocentrism, and historical insensitivity. The same phenomenon occurs with the word *post-modernism* as a designation of the art and literature of the United States and other countries. What is saddest—and most amusing—is that these terms, with the particular meaning attributed to them by Anglo-American critics, are beginning to be used not only in various European countries but also in Latin America and Spain. The point I am making is not uselessly polemic, nor does it reflect any sort of hackneyed chauvinism: the question of *modernism* is not a debate over words but over meanings, concepts, ideas of history. The world is a world of names. If the names are taken away from us, our world is taken away from us.

For the ancients, the great era of the past was the Golden Age, the Eden we left; for the moderns, the promised land was the future; but it is the present that has always been the time of poets and lovers, epicureans and mystics. The present is the moment of pleasure but also the moment of death, the time of the senses and the time of the revelation of the beyond. I believe that the new star—the one which has yet to appear on the historical horizon, but which has already been foretold in many indirect ways—will be the star of the present, the star of *now*. Men and women will soon have to construct an Ethics, a Politics, an Erotics, and a Poetics of the now. The path to the present passes through the body, but it need not and should not be confused with the mechanical and promiscuous hedonism of modern Western society. The present is the fruit in which life and death become one.

Poetry has always been the vision of a presence that reconciles the two halves of the globe. A plural presence: in the course of history it has changed its face and its name many times, and yet, throughout all these changes, it remains one. It has not been destroyed by the diversity of its manifestations. Even when it is identified with the void, as in the Buddhist tradition and among certain modern poets in the West, it appears, paradoxically, as a presence. It is not an idea: it is pure time. Time without measure. The singular, unique, particular time that is passing right now, and that has been passing endlessly from the beginning. Presence is the incarnation of the present.

On a number of occasions I have called the poetry of this time that is beginning: the art of convergence. And contrasted it with the tradition of rupture. "The poets of the modern age sought the principles of change; we poets of the age that is beginning seek the inalterable principle that is the root of all change. We wonder if the *Odyssey* and *A la recherche du temps perdu* do not have something in common. The aesthetics of change emphasized the historical character of the poem. Now we ask: Is there a point at which the principle of change will be fused with the principle of permanence? . . . The poetry that is beginning with this century's end does not really begin, nor does it return to its starting point; it is a perpetual re-beginning and a continual return. The poetry that is beginning now, without beginning, is seeking the intersection of times, the point of convergence. It asserts that between the cluttered past and the uninhabited future, poetry is the present." I wrote those words fifteen years ago. Today I would add: the present is manifest in presence, and presence is the reconciliation of the three times. A poetry of reconciliation: the imagination made flesh in a *now* that has no dates.

MEXICO CITY, AUGUST 12, 1986

Poetry, Myth,
Revolution

*Revolution confirms superstition
through sacrifice.*
—*Charles Baudelaire*

It is very difficult to say in a few clear words what I feel:
emotion, gratitude, surprise. Above all, I am moved that
you have been kind enough, Mr. President, to award me
the Alexis de Tocqueville Prize in person. I shall never
forget your gesture. Your generous words touch me
deeply: I see in them that particularly precious sign of
friendship that a writer sometimes gives to another whose
language is different, even when those languages are as
close as Spanish and French. My gratitude, therefore, is

Acceptance speech on receiving from President François Mitterrand of
France the Alexis de Tocqueville Prize in 1989.

twofold: toward the head of state and toward the writer of French, a language whose literature has been my second spiritual homeland.

My thanks to the members of the jury of the Alexis de Tocqueville Foundation is tinged with a slight and most pleasant sensation of unreality. When Mr. Alain Peyrefitte was good enough to inform me of the jury's decision, my first reaction, I confess, was one of disbelief: Why choose me, a poet? I soon guessed the reason: on certain occasions, impelled as much by the chance events of my life as by the changes and upheavals in the world and in my country, I have participated in public life, and wrote a number of books on the history and politics of our time. Above and beyond the dubious merits of my writings, I imagine that the jury wished to pay tribute, by way of my person, to a writer from a continent frequently torn between an immobility forcibly imposed by despotism and a turmoil caused by opposing factions. And to pay tribute, also, to a fidelity. In fact, I have always tried to be faithful to the attitude exemplified by the work and the person of Alexis de Tocqueville, which may be summed up in these words: My freedom begins with the recognition of the freedom of others. At the dawn of the Modern Age, confronted by a spectacle that has since been repeated many times—the tyrant disguised as liberator—Chateaubriand wrote the following prophetic words:

The Revolution would have carried me along . . . but I saw
the first head paraded on the end of a pike, and I recoiled. I
shall never look on murder as an argument in favor of liberty.
I know of nothing more servile, more cowardly, more obtuse
than a terrorist. Did I not find, later on, that entire race of
Brutuses in the service of Caesar and his police?

Since my adolescence I have written poems, and have
never ceased writing them. My ambition was to be a poet
and nothing but a poet. In my books in prose it was my
intention to serve poetry, to justify and defend it, to explain
it to others and to myself. I soon discovered that the de-
fense of poetry, scorned in our century, was inseparable
from the defense of freedom. That is the source of my
interest in the political and social questions that have con-
vulsed our time. After the Second World War, I met André
Breton and his friends. I do not share many of Breton's
philosophical and aesthetic ideas, but my admiration for
him is still intense and intact. In his writings, as in his life,
freedom and poetry have the same fiery face, at once cap-
tivating and tempestuous. Like Chateaubriand at the other
end of the spectrum, Breton never mistook the tyrant for
the liberator. Freedom is not a philosophy, nor is it even an
idea. It is a movement of consciousness that leads us, at
certain moments, to utter one of two monosyllables: Yes or
No. In their brevity, lasting but an instant, like a flash of

lightning, the contradictory character of human nature stands revealed.

Throughout history, and under the most diverse circumstances, poets have participated in political life. I am not referring to poetry as an art in the service of a state, a church, or an ideology. We already know that this concept of poetry, as old as political and ideological power, has invariably produced the same results: states fall, churches break apart or petrify, ideologies vanish—but poetry remains. No, I am referring to the participation of the poet in civic life. Even in societies that did not know political freedom—ancient China, for instance—not a few poets contributed to the administration of public affairs. Many among them did not hesitate to censure the abuses of the Son of Heaven, and they suffered imprisonment, exile, and other punishments for their opinions. In the West, this tradition has been extremely vital and long-lived: I need hardly invoke the memory of the poets of Greece and Rome. Two of the greatest poets of our tradition, the Florentine Dante and the Englishman Milton, were also notable political thinkers. To the former we owe the treatise *On Monarchy,* and to the latter, bold arguments in favor of freedom of conscience, such as his celebrated defense of the right to divorce, or his criticism of the censorship decreed by Parliament, which he had the courage to deliver before Parliament itself.

Yet such historical precedents should not hide from us

the fact that there is an essential difference between these attitudes and the situation of modern poets. The Chinese poets censured the throne, but they belonged to the imperial bureaucracy. Almost all were high officials, and their censure formed part of the moral and intellectual tradition of Confucianism. Dante and Milton found themselves engaged in controversies in which politics could not be distinguished from religion. For both, the basis of their opinions lay in theology. They fought in this world with their eyes fixed on the next, with arguments that came from Eternity. Dante placed Brutus and Cassius, two enemies of the empire, in the very last circle of Hell, alongside the archtraitor Judas Iscariot. For him, the reality of this world was a copy of the greater reality of the world beyond. Political crimes, therefore, were to be judged by the divine tribunal. In the Greek city-states, by contrast, and in the Roman republic, religion had a lesser place. The questions that divided citizens were clearly political, untinged by theology. And yet our similarity to Greco-Roman antiquity is deceptive. It lacks a central element, the distinctive sign that marks the birth of the Modern Age: the idea of Revolution. This is an idea that could have emerged only in our time, for it is the heir of both Greece and Christianity, that is to say, of philosophy and the longing for redemption.

In no other historical period has the idea of Revolution possessed such magnetic attraction. Other civilizations and other societies experienced immense changes—uprisings, the fall of dynasties, fratricidal wars—but only their great religious upheavals can be compared to our fascination with Revolution. It is an idea that has hypnotized many minds and generations for over two centuries. It has been the North Star that has guided our pilgrimages, the secret sun that has illuminated and warmed the sleepless nights of many solitary men. In it the certainties of reason and the hopes of religious movements are joined.

Revolution, from the moment it appeared on the horizon of history, had a dual nature: it was at once the result of an act of reason and the consequence of an act of providence. Rational cause-and-effect and miracle, history and myth. Criticism, the offspring of reason in its most rigorous and lucid form, is Revolution's image—an image both creative and destructive. For as it destroys, it creates. Revolution is that moment when criticism is transformed into utopia, and when utopia is embodied in a few individuals and in deeds. The descent of reason to earth was a true epiphany. It was lived as such by its protagonists, and later by its interpreters—lived, not thought, even though Revolution, for almost all of them, was a consequence of certain rational postulates and the general evolution of society. Almost none of them suspected that they were present at a resurrection. The newness of Revolution seems absolute; it breaks with the past and establishes a regime that is rational, just, and radically different from the old one. And yet this absolute newness is actually a return to the primordial beginning, to the time of origins, before injustice, before the moment when, according to Rousseau, the first man marked off a piece of land and said, "This is mine." On that day inequality began, and with it discord and oppression, that is to say, history. In short, Revolution is an eminently historical act that nonetheless negates history. The new time that it ushers in is a restoration of original time. As the child of history and reason, Revolution is the offspring of linear, successive, and unrepeatable time. But as the child of myth, it moves in cyclical time, like the stars and the seasons. The nature of Revolution, then, is dual. We cannot think it except by separating its two elements and discarding the mythic as a foreign body—and we cannot live it except by uniting them. We think it as a phenomenon foreseen by reason; we live it as a mystery. The fascination of Revolution lies in this enigma.

The Modern Age broke the ancient link that joined poetry and myth, only to proceed immediately to link poetry to Revolution, to the idea that proclaimed the end of myth and thus became the central myth of modernity. The history of modern poetry, from Romanticism down to our own day, has been nothing but the history of its relations to that myth, a myth as clear and coherent as a proof in geometry, and as turbulent as the revelations of primal chaos. Inflamed, extreme relations ranging from seduction to revulsion, from loyalty to anathema, from idolatry to abjuration—the entire gamut of the two great passions: love and religion. Hölderlin's enthusiasm for the young Bonaparte, and his disillusionment at seeing him turn into the emperor Napoleon. Wordsworth's Girondist sympathies, and the horror Robespierre inspired in him. These are but two examples of the great swings in the response of German and English Romantics to the French Revolution. And this was repeated throughout the nineteenth century, in reaction to each revolutionary movement. In the twentieth century, they culminate in the waves of contradictory feelings—once again ranging from fanaticism to digust—that the prolonged influence of the Bolshevik Revolution generated throughout the world.

The adherence awakened by all revolutions can be explained by the need we humans feel to correct, to put an end to, our unfortunate condition. There are periods when this need grows more intense and more urgent, because of the disappearance of traditional beliefs. The old gods crumble, rotted away by superstition, debased by fanaticism, corroded by criticism. A tribe of phantoms emerges then among the ruins: they appear first as radiant ideas but soon are deified and transformed into dreadful idols. Although there are other explanations of the revolutionary phenomenon—economic, psychological, political—all of them, if they are not false, essentially depend on this basic fact. A faith that is born in a void left by exhausted beliefs, that feeds on the awareness of our misery as well as on the geometries of reason, is a tough, resistant faith. It obstinately closes its eyes to the incoherences of its doctrine and the atrocities of its leaders. In this respect, revolutionary faith resembles religious faith: neither the slaughter of September 1792 nor the butchery of the Saint Bartholomew's Day massacre nor Stalin's gulag could shake the conviction of the faithful. But there is a difference. Revolutionary beliefs are subject to the proof of time, whereas religious beliefs are untouched by time and change. Revolutions are historical, temporal phenomena. And time's criticism is irrefutable, since it is reality's criticism: it sets the evidence before us without any need to offer whys and wherefores. And what it shows us is that Revolution begins as a promise, dissipates its energy in feverish agitation, and freezes into a bloody dictatorship that is the antithesis of the fiery impulse that brought it into being. In all revolutionary movements, the sacred time of myth inexorably becomes the profane time of history.

After each failure, hope is reborn. Shelley's enthusiasm refutes Coleridge's disenchantment, and Heine writes *Concerning Germany* as a reply to Madame de Staël, with the intention of ridiculing the poets of the preceding generation who initially showed sympathy for the French Revolution but in time became its enemies. The cycle of adherence–denial–adherence is repeated for more than two centuries, first in Europe, then throughout the world. For modern revolutions, the poetic word has been at once prophecy, anathema, and elegy. Although the differences between the two great revolutionary prototypes (the French Revolution of 1789 and the Russian Revolution of 1917) are greater than their similarities, the sentiments they inspired obeyed the same affective rhythm of attraction and repulsion. In spite of the fact that the religious function of modern revolutions is invariably crushed by the eminently historical nature of those movements, the result has been the rebirth of similar dreams and chimeras in the next generation—or the adoption of personal mythologies.

And this is another difference between modern poetry and the poetry that came before it. The key to Dante's poem was Holy Scripture, the axis of universal analogy; Blake, on the other hand, invented a mythology out of scraps of Gnosticism and the Hermetic tradition. Many poets did the same. The beliefs of Nerval and Hugo, the theosophy of Yeats, the occultism of Breton. The reason for this apparent paradox is that the public religion of modernity has been Revolution, while its private religion has been poetry.

The critics of revolution have been those nostalgic for the old order, and liberals (in the broad sense of the word, which denotes not so much a doctrine as a philosophical and political tendency). The liberal criticism has been more effective than the reactionary criticism. It dismantled the ideological constructs of revolutions, stripped them of their religious masks, and revealed them in their historic, profane nakedness. Liberalism did not propose to replace these constructs with others. It is the very nature of the liberal tradition to be critical, and this has prevented it, unlike other great political philosophies, from proposing a meta-history. Metahistory is a domain that once belonged to religion, but liberalism, offering nothing in exchange, limited religion to the private sphere. It based freedom on the only foundation that was able to sustain it: the autonomy of conscience, and the recognition of the autonomy of conscience in others. Admirable, but terrifying, too, because it locked us inside a solipsism, it broke the bridge that connected *I* to *thou* and both to the third person: the other, others. Between liberty and fraternity there is no contradiction, only a distance—one that liberalism has been unable to do away with. Robespierre and Saint-Just wanted to found solidarity among citizens on virtue. But what is the foundation of virtue? The Jacobins, like their descendants the Bolsheviks, did not ask themselves this question. Or, rather, their answer was virtue by decree, which is terror. And terror can engender nothing but the irreconcilable fraternity between executioners and victims.

Democratic liberalism is a civilized mode of living together. In my view, it is the best of all those that political philosophy has conceived. Yet it leaves unanswered half the questions human beings ask themselves about fraternity, about origins and final ends, about the meaning and the value of existence. The Modern Age has exalted individualism and has been, therefore, the period of the scattering and isolation of personal awarenesses. Poets have been particularly sensitive to this void. In 1851, Baudelaire wrote in one of his notebooks:

> *The world will end. . . . I'm not saying it will be reduced to the buffoonish chaos of the South American republics or that we will perhaps return to a state of savagery. . . . No: machinery will have so Americanized us and progress will have so completely atrophied our spiritual faculties that nothing, not even the sanguine chimeras of the utopians, could possibly compare to those excellent results. . . . But universal ruin (or universal progress: the name matters little to me) will manifest itself not in political institutions, but instead in the debasement of our souls.*

Ninety years later, as if continuing Baudelaire's reflections, Eliot in one of his *Four Quartets* sees our world, which we think is driven by progress, as the interminable fall of the void into the void:

> *O dark dark dark. They all go into the dark,*
> *The vacant interstellar spaces, the vacant into the vacant,*
> *The captains, merchant bankers, eminent men of letters,*
> *The generous patrons of art, the statesmen and the rulers,*
> *Distinguished civil servants, chairmen of many committees,*
> *Industrial lords and petty contractors, all go into the dark,*
> *And dark the Sun and Moon, and the Almanach de Gotha*

And the Stock Exchange Gazette, the Directory of Directors,
And cold the sense and lost the motive of action.
And we all go with them, into the silent funeral.
Nobody's funeral, for there is no one to bury.

I could add more quotes, but these two are enough to illustrate the spiritual state of poets when confronted with the disaster of modernity. Baudelaire's reflection and Eliot's verses are a funereal counterpoint to the enthusiastic paeans of praise of Whitman and Hugo. All are examples of the splitting—or, better, the rending in two—of modern poetry, the tear that distinguishes it from the poetry of other times and other civilizations. Suspended between the two hands of time, between myth and history, modern poetry consecrates a fraternity born of the same sense of solitude as that of primitive man surrounded by an alien and hostile nature. The difference is that we now live that solitude not only as we confront the cosmos, but as we confront our fellows as well. Yet we know, each of us in his own room, that we are not really alone: fraternity bridges the void.

After a long period of political stagnation, ever at the edge of the precipice, always facing the specter of total war and the threat of the annihilation of the human race, we have witnessed in the last thirty years a series of changes, of portents of a new era that may be dawning. First of all, the myth of revolution has seen twilight gather in the very place of its birth, Western Europe, which today has recovered from the war and is prosperous, pledged to a liberal, democratic form of government in each of the countries of the European Community. Second, there has been a return to democracy in Latin America, although democracy still totters between the phantoms of populist demagogy and militarism, our two endemic diseases, and iron shackles of debt hang around its neck. Finally, there have been changes in the Soviet Union, and in other totalitarian regimes in Eastern and Central Europe. Whatever the scope of these reforms, they clearly signify the end of the myth of authoritarian socialism. The reforms are autocriticisms, tantamount to a confession. That is why I have spoken of the end of an era: the twilight of Revolution in its last, disastrous, Bolshevik incarnation. Revolution as an idea survives only in a few regions on the periphery, and among some crazed groups, such as the Peruvian terrorists. We do not know what the future holds: virulent nationalism, ecological catastrophe, the rebirth of buried mythologies, new fanaticisms. But also new discoveries, new creations—history and its retinue of horrors and marvels. We do not know whether the peoples of the Soviet Union will experience new forms of oppression or some original, Slavic version of democracy. In either case, the revolutionary myth is dying. Will it revive? I don't think so. A Holy Alliance is not killing it; it is dying a natural death.

Joyce said that history is a nightmare. He was mistaken;

a nightmare vanishes with the light of day, but history will not be over until our species has come to an end. We are human in and through history. If history ceased, we would cease to be human. But the end of the revolutionary myth will perhaps permit us to think again of the principles that have founded our society, and of its deficiencies and gaps. Relieved at last of the struggle against totalitarian superstition, we can now reflect more freely on our own tradition. And so the theme of the *virtue* of citizens again makes its appearance. It is a theme that has come down to us from classical antiquity. It concerned Machiavelli and Montesquieu, and today it has a painful actuality in many countries, including the Anglo-American democracy founded on the Puritan ethic. Kant taught us that ethics cannot be based on history, since history flows unceasingly and we do not know if any law or purpose rules its capricious course. We also know that metahistorical constructs—whether religious or metaphysical, conservative or revolutionary— strangle liberty and eventually corrupt fraternity. The thought of the era that is beginning—if, in fact, an era is beginning—will of necessity have to find the point of convergence between liberty and fraternity. We must rethink our tradition, renovate it, and seek to reconcile the two great political traditions of modernity: liberalism and socialism. I will go so far as to say, paraphrasing Ortega y Gasset, that this is "the theme of our time." It seems to me that our era favors such a vast undertaking. In certain contemporary authors—in the work, for example, of Cornelius Castoriadis—I detect the beginning of a response.

What can the contribution of poetry be in the creation of a new political theory? Not new ideas, but something more precious and fragile: memory. In each generation, poets rediscover the terrible antiquity—and the no less terrible youth—of passion. In schools and universities where the so-called political sciences are taught, the reading of Aeschylus and Shakespeare ought to be obligatory. Poets nourished the thought of Hobbes and Locke, of Marx and Tocqueville. Through the mouth of the poet there speaks—I emphasize speaks, not writes—the *other* voice. It is the voice of the tragic poet and the buffoon, the voice of solitary melancholy and merrymaking, of laughter and sighs, the voice of the lovers' embrace and of Hamlet's contemplation of the skull, the voice of silence and tumult, mad wisdom and wise madness, the intimate whispers of the bedroom and the uproar of the crowd in the square. To hear that voice is to hear time itself, the time that passes but comes back, transformed into a few crystalline syllables.

MEXICO CITY, JUNE 1989

Poetry and
the End of
the Century

The Few and
the Many

Every reflection on poetry should begin, or end, with this
question: How many people read books of poems, and
who are they? I have deliberately used the word *poems*,
not poetry, because one can argue endlessly about what
poetry is but it is not difficult to agree on the meaning of
the word *poem*: a thing made of words, for the purpose of
containing and secreting a substance that is impalpable,
resistant to definition, and called poetry. The question has
two parts and borders both on statistics—How many?—
and on sociology: What sort of men and women read
poems? Confronted with a similar question, Juan Ramón
Jiménez answered with the dedication to one of his books:

"To the immense minority." *Minority* reduces the number of readers to Stendhal's "happy few," but *immense* abruptly increases it: the few are many—so many that they are uncountable, like everything that is immense. Jiménez places in opposition the countable majority and a minority that cannot be counted. A logical impossibility, because the minority, if it is uncountable, cannot be a minority, and if it is countable, it cannot be immense. Moreover, if the minority is uncountable, then the majority must be, too. Two immensities, two infinities? That would be too many: one infinity is enough to overwhelm us and do away with us.

The sentence may have another meaning: the readers of poems, always few though many, participate individually and collectively in the immense. And what is the immense? That which has no measure, or that which is impossible to measure. The many/few who read poems worm their way into immeasurable realities, and in the mirrors of words discover their own infinity. The reading of a poem connects the reader with a realm that is transpersonal and, therefore, in the strict sense of the word, immense. The connection, almost always, is brief. Sometimes it fits into six words: "D'altri diluvi una colomba ascolto" [I hear a dove from other floods].*

But whether there be few or many, it is not likely that

*Giuseppe Ungaretti, "Una Colomba" (1925). The whole poem.

the readers of poems have ever constituted the majority of a society, except perhaps at the dawn of history or in communities that we call primitive. According to certain ethnologists, until just a few years ago men and women in the jungles of equatorial America gathered at nightfall around a campfire to listen, in fascination, to the stories of the gods and the genealogy of the tribe. Through myths, which are the substance of these poetic accounts, each member of the group felt that he was a part of a totality at once natural and supernatural, because the dead ancestors were also members of the tribe. The recitation by campfire light of poems recounting the origin of the world and of the ethnos made the relation between the two live and, in the strict sense of the word, real. The tribe, for an hour or two, turned into a true poetic community that encompassed the living and the dead.

However, since the beginning of history—that is, since human beings abandoned their Neolithic villages and began to live in cities—the original collective was fragmented: divided into classes, occupations, and groups— day laborers, craftsmen, soldiers, priests, lords, monarchs. Even religious beliefs were divided; the potter's faith was not the theologian's faith, the scribe's was not the slave's. The division of society corresponded to the existence now of arts, sciences, and technology. In the time before time, poetry and religion, science and magic, song and dance were one and the same thing. As each art became autonomous and each branch of knowledge separate, groups, traditions, and audiences also became fragmented. The plurality of subcultures within a culture is indicative of the coexistence of different minorities, some of them lovers of poetry, others of music, others of astronomy. These minorities are relative and variable, by which I mean that at times they may become majorities, even though only for a short while. In this instance, as in so many others, statistics are an illusion: Many and few, majority and minority, are notions that have no fixed boundaries.

The coexistence of various minorities does not exclude—on the contrary, it includes—communication between them. The network of relationships between different groups forms an impalpable but real fabric: the culture of a people. Above each subculture—and below it, too—are ideas, beliefs, and customs common to all members of the society. It is the basis—spiritual, mental, and emotional—of a people; it is also the foundation of the arts, especially of poetry. An inexhaustible fountainhead. People recognize themselves in works of art because the works of art offer them images of the hidden totality. Even when they express the dispersion and the atomization of a society and individuals, as happens in modern poetry and novels, they still speak of the lost community. Hence it is not so important that a work is read in the beginning by only a few. The preservation of the collective memory by a group, even a small one, is a true tablet of salvation for the entire community. It is by means of such tablets that traditions and cultures cross the seas of time.

Apart from this community of beliefs and images—what used to be called "the soul of peoples"—there are subjects, episodes, and characters that at a more superficial level move multitudes and take possession of the collective imagination. These are "public affairs": religious and political ideas, quarrels over beliefs and institutions, movements of opinion in this or that direction. Public affairs are also events, news, names: coronations, religious or civic celebrations, falls of dynasties, revolts and insurrections, marriages of royalty, regicides, the death of chieftains, and so on. A private incident can become a public one: the love affair of an actress, the suicide of a banker, a robbery, a murder, the sudden wealth or unexpected poverty of this individual or that, the prowess of a champion, and finally, all the prodigious turns of the wheel of fortune. No writer, including the authors of today's best-sellers, has attained the fame of an Attila or a Napoleon, the popularity of a Jack Dempsey or a Marilyn Monroe. There is, of course, the case of Lope de Vega in the seventeenth century, Voltaire in the eighteenth, Victor Hugo in the nineteenth, Picasso in our day, and a handful of others. But apart from the fact that they are a handful, these exceptions prove the rule.

It is natural, and the preeminence in the popular imagination of leaders, kings, presidents, movie stars, television personalities, and famous figures in the world of sports should come as no surprise. What is extraordinary is that human beings, since the beginning of time, should compose poems, paint pictures, carve stone sculptures or cast them in bronze, model in clay, and invent stories with words. And it is no less extraordinary that these works endure and are transmitted from generation to generation. Technology changes—printing replaces the manuscript and television may perhaps do away with books (I doubt it very much)—but the arts, whatever the technology and the state of society, endure. Public affairs and their preeminent figures pass; poems, paintings, and symphonies do not. The permanence of the arts—and the same can be said of the sciences and philosophy—has always been the work of a minority. My conclusion: the numerical question—How many: a lot or a few?—is meaningless by itself. In order to be meaningful, the question must be put in a context in which two terms are involved. These terms are division in space, that is, the plurality of publics and audiences, and continuity in time, that is, the unbroken succession of generations of readers and listeners. Neither diversity nor continuity is a purely numerical concept.

I am afraid that my reasoning will not convince many people. For the modern mentality, no argument is worth as much as a number. Sociologists, academics, journalists, and managing editors tell us that they are armed with irrefutable statistics. Pointing to statistics, they maintain that poetry is an art destined to disappear or become yet another curiosity in the museum of antiques. They have boldly formulated a sort of law of the progressive decline of poetry: poems have fewer readers today than they did thirty years ago, and thirty years ago they had fewer readers than they did seventy years ago, and so on, back through time. But in this domain, as in almost any other, the quantitative criterion alone is insufficient. Is such a conclusion correct? Let us look and see. A few days ago, I bought a little volume in a New York City bookstore: *The Best American Poetry, 1989.* The book is an anthology of the best poems written in the United States in 1988. Its editor is the poet and critic Donald Hall. In the foreword, Hall touches on the same subject as these pages of mine, and he produces facts and figures. I reproduce some of his data below. Although they speak for themselves, I have seen fit to add certain comments.

Hall begins by pointing out, as a sign of the vitality of poetry, the revival of the custom of poets reading their own works aloud before large audiences. The practice began around 1950, became popular during the following decade, and has grown increasingly popular ever since. To understand the significance of this fact, I must mention something that, although common knowledge, is almost always forgotten: at the beginning of our civilization (as well as in the Far East), poems were recited and sung. The *aoidos* was the epic poet of ancient Greece, and the word comes from the verb *aeidein:* to sing. A rhapsody was a poem or a fragment of an epic poem; the rhapsode was a wandering singer who recited epic songs, particularly those of Homer. Lyric poetry was also recited to the accompaniment of a musical instrument, among both Greeks and Romans. This has been a general custom and appears in all societies, in the Orient as well as in pre-Columbian America. In Europe it was preserved for more than fifteen hundred years, and it is hardly necessary to call to mind the minstrels, jongleurs, and madrigalists or the reading aloud of poems in patrician houses before a select group of members of the family, intimate friends, and courtiers. In the nineteenth century, reading aloud was supplanted by individual reading in silence: the triumph of the book and of writing. In the first third of the twentieth century, the custom of reading poetry aloud disappeared almost entirely.

Hall observes that between 1920 and 1950, one of the great periods of modern poetry in the United States, not only were public readings rare, but very seldom did famous poets—Frost, Eliot, Pound—participate in them. But at the end of the 1950s, with the sudden appearance of the Beat generation, this changed, and public readings are now one of the characteristic features of literary life in the United States. Today they are part of the cultural calendar, along with exhibitions, concerts, and dance performances. The frequency of such events in any one week is surprising, both in major cities and at universities. The audience is usually made up of young people, which means that this is not a custom that is dying out—as prophets of the end of poetry maintain—but a living tradition, one that is being taken up again and renewed. Some tell me that neither in Latin America nor in Europe, with the exception of England, are public poetry readings as frequent and as well attended as in the United States. That is true. It is also true that in Russia such readings are even more popular than in the United States.

In 1950, Hall says, an edition of a book of a poet already known to the public—his second or third book— had a printing of a few hundred copies; today it has four or five thousand. The books of major poets or those with a solid reputation easily sell ten thousand copies, and several have gone as high as fifty thousand. A few years ago, *Publishers Weekly* put out a list of best-sellers that included biographies, books on current affairs, novels, travel books and cookbooks, works on sexology, and many other genres—but it did not include books of poems. At the head of the list was *The Joy of Sex,* which sold in the millions; lower on the scale were titles that had had sales of 250,000 copies. In that same year, the poet Lawrence Ferlinghetti sold a million copies of *A Coney Island of the Mind,* and Allen Ginsberg's *Howl,* around that time, had sales that easily topped a million copies. Yet *Publishers Weekly* did not include them on the list. Because they were books of poems? These two cases are unusual, I grant you, but many contemporary poets, even though the sales of their books do not reach a million, are read by thirty thousand readers or more. Among those books are a number originally written in other languages, by such poets as García Lorca, Rilke, or Neruda. I spare my reader Hall's other figures, though not his conclusion: the number of readers of poems has increased ten times in the course of the last thirty years. This means that there are ten times more readers of poems today than during the period of the preeminence of great poets like Eliot, Pound, Williams, and Stevens, which was a superb monument in the history of twentieth-century poetry. That is impressive.

Hall's statistics refer only to living poets of the United States. Do they have an equivalent in other countries? I do not know. But it is not throwing caution to the winds to presume that the number of readers of poems in the Soviet Union has increased even more than in the United States. As much can be said of Japan, a nation whose poetic tradition has been outstanding. It is equally certain that the number of readers of poems in Europe has increased, at least in England, the Scandinavian countries, Poland, and Hungary. And in Mexico, too, though we are a country of few readers: fifty years ago, the editions of our poets—Pellicer, Gorostiza, Villaurrutia—had printings of five hundred copies.

But what about quality? In all languages and in all periods, the volumes of poetry that really count are very few. Isn't the same true of other genres, the novel in particular? Every year, publishers launch thousands upon thousands of novels whose brightly colored covers fill the windows of bookstores. In a few weeks they disappear without a trace. They are not birds but books of passage. Academics and university presses, at the other extreme from commercial publishing houses, also contribute to what can only be called the literary traffic jam. The recent boom of the criticism industry in universities has turned the modest mounds of trash that literature left behind into veritable Himalayas of refuse.

Hall's figures are consoling, but they lose significance when one notices that the increase in readership is a phenomenon that encompasses all the genres. People today read more than ever, yes. But do they read better? I doubt it. Distraction is our habitual state. Not the distraction of the person who withdraws from the world in order to shut himself up inside the secret and ever-changing land of his fantasy, but the distraction of the person who is always outside himself, lost in the trivial, senseless turmoil of everyday life. A thousand things bid for our attention at the same time, but none manages to hold our interest; thus life turns to sand between our fingers and hours to smoke in our brains. If we had the courage to make a daily examination of our acts and thoughts, we would confess that we are guilty not of inexpiable crimes but of countless momentary desires and appetites followed by momentary renunciations or betrayals of ourselves and others. But are we even able to remember what we did yesterday? If our sin goes by the name of dissipation, our punishment goes by the name of forgetfulness. Reading is the opposite of dissipation; it is a mental and moral practice of concentration which leads us to unknown worlds. Worlds that little by little reveal themselves to be an older, truer homeland: we came from there. To read is to discover unsuspected paths that lead to our own selves. It is a recognition. In the era of advertising and instantaneous communication, how many people are able to read in this way? Very few. But the continuity of our civilization lies in them, not in the data of statistical surveys.

By themselves, facts and figures are not an answer to our question; but they help to define it, to phrase it more precisely. It is useful to compare Hall's statistics, limited to his country and the contemporary period, with statistics from other countries and periods. The poet and critic Pere Gimferrer deals with this subject in an essay that is both intelligent and full of information: "La poesía y el libro."* In Gimferrer's view, one of the main features of modern poetry is its determination to remain an art for a minority. In the first half of the last century, the great European Romantics did their best to win over a vast public of faithful readers. A number of them, such as Byron, Hugo,

---

*"Poetry and Publishing." Included in the collective volume *La cultura del libro* (Madrid, 1988).

and Lamartine, succeeded. Later, as the great Romantic conflagration subsided, poets withdrew from the public eye. And since the great Symbolists, poetry has been an act of solitary rebellion, an underground subversion of language or of history. None of the poets who ushered in modernity sought the approval of the crowd. On the contrary, they deliberately chose to write in a way that "contravened the public's taste." Rimbaud and his heirs in the first half of the twentieth century exemplify one aspect of this tendency; its other, more purely aesthetic expression can be found in Mallarmé and his followers.

It is hard not to agree with Gimferrer. But I would point out that his line of reasoning is based mainly on the history of modern French poetry; in other languages, the will to break with public taste does not always make an appearance. Neither Tennyson nor Browning, in Victorian England, followed the French in their rigorous subversive efforts and in their aesthetic asceticism. Tennyson and Browning were much more widely read than the French Symbolists. A similar statement might be made concerning Germany, and Russia, Poland, and the other Slavic nations. In the countries whose language was Spanish, little reading took place—not because poets derided the taste of the bourgeoisie, but because of the intellectual inertia that came over Spain and its former colonies at the turn of the last century. But it is misleading to compare the French poetry of the last third of the nineteenth century with that of other languages. French poetry lived, as poetry, in another time: it marks the beginning of our poetry of today. Mallarmé and Tennyson were contemporaries, but Tennyson belongs to the nineteenth century and Mallarmé to the twentieth. It is also true that the poetry that is the origin of our own century often manifested itself in a way different from—even opposed to—that of a Rimbaud or a Mallarmé. Instead of withdrawing from the world, it may have sought to be one with the man in the street. I am thinking of Walt Whitman in particular.

Gimferrer's statistics are no less surprising than Hall's, though in an opposite way. In 1886, Verlaine published the second edition of one of his most famous books, *Fêtes galantes*. Six hundred copies were printed, of which a hundred were set aside for the author and reviewers. A revealing fact, because by 1886 Verlaine was already a famous poet, and not just in France: he was read avidly all over Europe, and revered in Buenos Aires and Mexico City.* In 1876, Mallarmé brought out a deluxe edition of *L'Après-midi d'un faune:* 195 copies. Eleven years later, in 1887, *Poésies* appeared, an anthology of his poems that he himself selected: this edition numbered forty copies. As for Rim-

---

*I made a brief investigation of my own and discovered that up to the time of Verlaine's death in 1896, the first editions of his books usually did not go beyond six hundred copies, and the second editions eleven hundred.

baud, in 1873 he himself paid for the publication of the first edition of *Une saison en enfer,* a text that has had, as we know, an enormous influence on twentieth-century poetry. The edition was limited to five hundred copies. Rimbaud kept six for himself; the rest would have disappeared in the printer's storerooms had it not been for a bibliophile who rescued them in 1901, although he did not announce his find until 1914. The fate of Rimbaud's other great work, *Illuminations,* is no less bizarre: Verlaine published it, with a brief foreword, in 1886, in the review *La Vogue,* and then later that same year in a slim *plaquette.* Rimbaud, in Abyssinia at the time, was completely unaware of either publication. Lautréamont, too, paid the costs of publication of his book, *Les Chants de Maldoror.* The edition was never distributed and lay forgotten in the publisher's cellar until Léon Bloy and Rémy de Gourmont, many years after the author's death, enthusiastically undertook the task of drawing attention to this sumptuous, lugubrious work.*

Gimferrer gives a number of similar examples of books of poetry in Spanish. Especially dramatic is Neruda's *Veinte poemas de amor y una canción desesperada.* This small volume, published in Santiago, Chile, in 1924, was entirely unknown in Spain, despite the fact that by 1936 Neruda

---

*Among the exceptions Gimferrer cites, the most notable is Byron's *Corsair:* ten thousand copies sold the first day! For that era, says Gimferrer, a phenomenon comparable to the popularity of the Beatles.

was an established poet throughout the Spanish-speaking world. Altolaguirre decided to bring out a new edition of the book under a different title: *Primeros poemas de amor*. Five hundred copies were printed. And I can add two examples, which are no less sad than Rimbaud's and Lautréamont's: Gutiérrez Nájera and Silva died without ever seeing their poems brought together in a book. And how many copies of the first two editions of *Azul* were printed? Or of the first edition of *Prosas profanas*? Or of Díaz Mirón's *Lascas,* brought out in Jalapa by the official press of the state of Veracruz? Or of Vallejo's *Los heraldos negros* and *Trilce*? And another example, this one Italian: the first edition of what was to become one of the essential books of Italian poetry in this century, Ungaretti's *L'allegria* (1915), consisted of eighty copies. The list could go on ad libitum and would include our best-known and most widely read poets.

At this point, the question arises: The scant number of copies, is it due to a decision on the part of the poets or to the indifference of the public? Both. Poetry, from its very beginning, has had an ambiguous relationship with modernity, as I have attempted to show elsewhere in my writings.* But the conflict between poet and public became bitter at the end of the last century and turned into open

---

El arco y la lira, and especially *Los hijos del limo*. (For English translation information, see footnotes on page 1.)

dissidence during the period of the avant-gardes, in the first third of our century. Poetry disdained and frequently mocked traditional values, both moral and aesthetic. It undermined language. It threw signs and meanings into confusion, and invented worlds inhabited by fascinating verbal monsters, worlds that had deceptively transparent pools into which consciousness could plunge to its death. The public's indifference was the reaction of a social class, the bourgeoisie, which embodied the modernity at once desired and despised by the poets. This class saw itself reviled first by the Romantics, then by the Symbolists, and finally by the various avant-garde movements. Its antipathy toward modern art was encouraged by hostile academic criticism and the malevolence of ignorant journalists and reviewers. Nevertheless, as will be seen, poetry's dissidence was never absolute, and poetry was and remains a necessity.

The first edition of *Les Fleurs du mal* in 1857 had a printing of eleven hundred copies, and it was some time before it was sold out. The second edition, four years later, was a more resounding success, no doubt because of the court order telling the publisher to suppress a number of poems judged to be immoral. Baudelaire did not lack defenders, among them Hugo and Gautier; in addition two young poets, Mallarmé and Verlaine, hailed him in reviews for youthful literati and proclaimed him their maestro. But this recognition was late in coming: Baudelaire had already suffered his first attack of hemiplegia and died two years later. Following his death in 1867, editions followed one after the other, without interruption, as did translations into almost every language. Baudelaire died more than a century ago, but he is our contemporary. His work would share the same good fortune as that of Verlaine, Rimbaud, and Mallarmé: the books of these poets can be found in any library, and are read by thousands upon thousands of cultivated people. In 1855, the first edition of *Leaves of Grass* appeared, without the name of the author but with a portrait sketch of Whitman on the title page. A year later, the second edition was published, and it was followed by others, nine in all, each with additional poems, until his death in 1892. The first edition consisted of 795 copies. Whitman not only paid the costs of publication himself but was also the printer. Until the fifth edition, he did not make a single penny of profit, and from the fifth he earned—twenty-five dollars! But Whitman, unlike so many other nineteenth-century poets, was able to see, in the course of less than half a century, successive editions of his book winning him fervent readers, among whom were major writers: his countrymen Emerson and Thoreau; and later Swinburne and Tennyson in England. Oscar Wilde visited Whitman in 1882, and in 1886 Thomas Eakins painted his portrait.

The histories of the editions of Baudelaire and Whitman are the same for all modern poets, in every language. The first edition is almost always paid for by the author and meant for a circle of intimates, yet by a process that is slow but sure, his books eventually attain large printings and reach large audiences. The works of Rubén Darío, Antonio Machado, Federico García Lorca, and other poets who wrote in Spanish not only amount to many thousands of copies today but also are continually appearing in new editions. The phenomenon occurs regardless of the country, whether the poet is Apollinaire or Rilke, Montale or Mandelshtam. Reprintings of Yeats and Eliot are frequent, and the number of copies now goes as high as a hundred thousand. The young critic Edward Mendelson, to whom we owe the outstanding edition of all Auden's poems, told me a short time ago that the popular reprintings of this poet vary between forty and fifty thousand copies. What strikes me as significant in all these examples is not so much the number of copies as the continuity. The best-seller, be it a novel or a book on current affairs, appears on the scene like a meteor: everyone rushes to buy it, but in a short time it disappears forever. The best-sellers that manage to survive their own success are few and far between. Best-sellers are not works of literature, they are merchandise. What distinguishes a literary work from a book that is merely entertaining or informative is the fact that the latter is meant literally to be consumed by its readers, whereas the former has the ability to come back to life. Poetry seeks not immortality but resurrection.

Sometimes a historical change—whether in matters of

taste, ideas, or social conviction—may condemn to purgatory a poet who was celebrated during his lifetime. Neruda, Aragon, and Eluard, for example, are now paying for their political sins. I say "sins," because Stalinism was more than a mere error, it was a moral wrong. But as Auden himself wrote, apropos of Yeats—whether out of resignation or cynicism, I cannot say—these poets will again be read, for the mastery of their art:

> Time that with this strange excuse
> Pardoned Kipling and his views,
> And will pardon Paul Claudel,
> Pardons him for writing well.

The disparity between the first reception of books of poems and their later fortune calls for comment. The transition from hostility or indifference to appreciation has never been instantaneous; it requires time. In this case, time means culture, in the primary sense of the term: the reader must become cultivated. And cultivation, every kind, produces change and transformation. Each new poetic work challenges the public's mind and taste. To appreciate it, a reader must learn the vocabulary of the work and assimilate its syntax. This means unlearning the known and learning the new; the unlearning/learning implies an intimate renewal, a change of sensibility and vision. The experience is not peculiar to the Modern Age. The courtiers and clerics of seventeenth-century England had to learn the language of the so-called Metaphysical Poets, and Spaniards of that same century had to learn the language of Góngora and his followers. The phenomenon is repeated in every era and in all societies. The quarrel over form and artistic language is almost always linked to the struggle between generations: the old and the new, age and youth.

The present situation is even more complex. In addition to the traditional dispute between the old and the new, there is a more profound opposition, one of a historical, spiritual nature. As I suggested above, it has to do with the rift between poetry, the rebel against modernity, and the bourgeoisie, which was the creator and at the same time the consummate, most dynamic product of modernity. How was it possible for this opposition, which began with Romanticism and has continued to our own day, to turn into interludes of harmony—followed by new ruptures? Every period is different, just as the relationship between every reader and every poem is different, but it is not foolhardy to offer a general explanation. I will put it before you very briefly. From Romanticism on, poets have been the rebellious offspring of modernity; as they wound it, they exalt it. Readers mirror this ambivalence, recognizing themselves in both the wound and the exaltation, for they, too, are the offspring of modernity, linked to it by the same detested filial ties. Modern poetry, precisely because it is modern, has criticized and is criticizing modernity, and its readers recognize themselves in it for the same reason. Since its birth, modernity has been locked in combat with itself. This is the source of its ambiguity, the secret of its continual transformation and change. Modernity emits criticism the way an octopus emits ink. This criticism, unfailingly, turns against itself.

Quantity and
Quality

This reflection began with a question divided into two parts. The first was quantitative: How many readers of poems are there? As we have seen, this numerical part of the question by itself is meaningless. The number of readers varies with different societies and periods, and varies within each period; it varies even for the same poet. The esoteric, unreadable Eliot, read by a clique of eccentrics in 1920, in 1940 becomes Bishop Eliot, who is listened to worshipfully by multitudes. *How many?*, to make sense, must be considered together with the second part of the question: *Who?* What sort of people read books of poems? The *Who?* includes the *How many?* Or, rather, it dilutes it, so that the number ceases to be a number. The question *Who?* implies, first, a plurality of places: Where, the country, the city? And it introduces the dimension of time: When, which century, what year? And finally, the where and when are related to social class, political and religious affiliation, and an economy, a culture. The where and when turn into a history. The nature of the public that reads or listens to poems is a historical question. An awesomely large subject, and one impossible to explore in an essay of this type. But it is altogether possible to point out certain ideas, to outline some sort of hypothesis. My aim here is more modest: to offer a few suggestions and conjectures, in the hope that they will prompt someone to write, in the not too distant future, a study of the state of poetry as the twentieth century draws to a close.

I begin at the very beginning, with Homer, who is the origin of Greece and therefore of our poetry. His great poems, his heroes, and his moral code were the aesthetic and ethical archetypes for Greeks and Romans. In a manner of speaking, the *Iliad* and the *Odyssey* were the Bible and Vedas of the Hellenes. Children and adolescents, as they learned arithmetic or exercised at the gymnasium, also recited the ancient hexameters. In the grandiose endeavor to Hellenize Rome, it was absolutely necessary that there be a poetic founding text equivalent to the Homeric poems. But the *Aeneid,* written at the zenith of Rome's history, was not so much a creation as a re-creation, not an origin but a consecration. During the Middle Ages and the Renaissance, the educational function of Virgil's poem was analogous to that of the Homeric poems in antiquity. In China the *Shih Ching* (Book of Songs), an anthology of ancient poems compiled by Confucius, had the same civilizing influence. In Japan this mission was fulfilled by the *Manyoshu* (The Ten-Thousand-Leaf Collection) and the great anthologies that followed it. Poetry as the founding Word of a people is a feature that appears in every civilization, from the poem of Gilgamesh, the probable source of our epic tradition, to that of the Cid. In other cultures, poetry was intimately associated not only with religion and mythology but also with the other arts. We know, for instance, that the Aztecs recited, sang, and what is even more noteworthy, danced their poems. Another feature common to ancient societies: the confraternities, brotherhoods, orders of poets. These groups frequently fulfilled religious and liturgical functions. Among many peoples, poets were regarded as clairvoyants and soothsayers. It was widely believed that the poet knew the future because he knew the past. His knowledge was the knowledge of origins. In such societies, the present and the future are both functions, in the mathematical sense of the word, of the past.

The collections of poetic texts, true founding writings, constituted what our secular society today calls a *classical canon*. Without these poems it is impossible to know and understand their societies. The aesthetic, ethical, and philosophical influence they exerted was immense. In Greece, tragedy was nurtured by the epic, both its conflicts and its heroes. Similarly, philosophy began as a critique of Homer, of his theology and moral code. The classical canon was transmitted through the education of adolescents: poetry was a principal subject in the curriculum of the young. Thus, alongside civic and religious education, and exercises in preparation for combat, poetry was an initiation into adult life and its two great facets: action and contemplation. Citizen, patrician, *eques,* mandarin, *tecuhtli,* and other social groups and categories that managed the affairs of ancient societies in both peace and war—all were educated, formed by a poetic tradition that inspired their public discourse and their public action.

The influence of poetry was equally profound in private life: eroticism, friendship, piety in the form of mercy toward one's unfortunate fellow man (Achilles face-to-face with Priam), solitude, the bitter pleasures of melancholy, the fragile realm of memory. Poets helped us to know what the passions were, and hence to know ourselves: envy, sensuality, cruelty, hypocrisy—in short, all the complexity of the human soul. The first great love poem of the West dates from the third century B.C.: Theocritus's pointed tale of the sensual and ingenuous, rabid and sublime love of the ill-starred young Simetha. Later, in Rome, Catullus and Propertius shed light on the dark corners of love and discovered the insidious power of that fatal passion, jealousy. Without Catullus and Propertius, Shakespeare might not have been able to conceive Othello, or Proust to discover Swann's torment. From the feudal era to that of the bourgeoisie, poetry continued to inspire warriors and lovers: Parsifal and Roland, courtly love and Petrarchism, libertines and Romantics. One of the roots of contemporary feminism may be found in the "courts of love" of the twelfth century. As in antiquity and in the East, poetry also nurtured philosophers. There is scarcely one of our great thinkers, from Saint Thomas to Machiavelli, from Bacon to Schopenhauer, from Montaigne to Karl Marx, who has not written poems, or whose writings are not embellished with verses and maxims taken from poets. Seen from this perspective, the numerical question disappears. We do not know how many Romans read Ovid, how many Italians Petrarch, or how many of the French Ronsard, but we know *who* read them. And these readers, whether few or many, were the head and heart of society, its thinking and acting nucleus. Although they belonged to the ruling classes, many were dissidents, critics of the status quo. Some were recluses, intellectual hermits.

The change began in the last years of the nineteenth century. After the great pitched battles of Romanticism, poetry retreated underground: clandestine war, conspiracy in the catacombs. But as we have seen, this retreat was a victory: yesterday's poets, cursed and bound for Hell, are today's patron saints. The displacement of the humanities, which are no longer the center of our educational systems, has had even graver consequences. A sign of the times: Baudelaire wrote a poem in Latin, Rimbaud won first prize in Latin composition in his lycée, and Lautréamont studied literary precepts in a treatise by José Gómez Hermosilla, a severe classicist and a remarkable translator of the *Iliad*— but Whitman, the first great modern poet, never went through a university or took a course in the humanities. Loss or gain? I would say that the gain compensates for the loss. And Whitman carries on a different tradition, one no less venerable than the Greco-Latin: the tradition based on the Bible.

Today the sciences occupy the place of Latin and Greek. The change has been natural and justified. But the preeminence of *scientism,* a modern superstition, has been less natural and is totally unjustified. Each science may speak with authority with regard to its particular domain: there is no such thing as Science; there are only sciences. But scientism would translate the discourse of physics, chemistry, or biology into human domains: history, society, the individual, the passions. One could ask: Is the practice of the various sciences possible without the common store of wisdom that is represented by the humanities? Perhaps, but the cost is immense. Neither Freud nor Einstein forgot the classics.

The proliferation of the social sciences is even more

dangerous than the scientistic superstition. I refer not to the
real value of these sciences, which is estimable, despite the
frailty of their methods and the uncertainty of their conclu-
sions, but to the misuse of them by ideologues wearing the
mask of professor or scientific researcher. The harm done
has been twofold: political and aesthetic. Our classics, apart
from their being examples of formal perfection and sources
of spiritual pleasure, were teachers of political wisdom for
two millennia. Today this function is fulfilled by professors
of sociology and so-called political science. The majority of
these people are ignorant of the classical heritage, or scorn
it. Firmly seated on their dogmas, they impart from their
university chairs formulas that explain any and every social
phenomenon save that of their own peculiar position in the
modern world. In the name of modernity, they have been
the spokesmen—and sometimes the middlemen—of a new
political and intellectual obscurantism. Intolerant sophists,
they are unworthy heirs of the Enlightenment. In recent
days we have been witness to dramatic changes in those
European countries living under the regime of "bureau-
cratic socialism." It would be futile to search through the
writings of the professors for the slightest premonition of
these prodigious changes, for that matter, or an explanation
today of their cause. In order to find coherent critics who
foresaw what is happening now, it is necessary to reread the
texts of the dissidents and the excommunicated. The pro-
fessors' blindness comes from their faith in ideologies, the

domain of illusory certitudes, and from their disdain for history, which is subject to chance and the unpredictable. Classical literature, on the other hand, is thoroughly imbued with the random nature of historical events. Machiavelli and Montesquieu, Tocqueville and Marx profited from their reading of the poets and historians of antiquity. What do academic politicologues read today, if anything? There are exceptions, of course, but still they are exceptions.

The application of the methods of the natural sciences to the study of society and social change has not had, so far, the results hoped for. Despite this failure, smug and thoroughly confused theorists have decided to extend the scientific method to literature as well. They forget that different realities require different methods, different criteria. The transformation of a cell is not the same thing as the transformation of a society; nor does social change suffice to explain change in the realm of art and literature. The creative work is reduced to nothing more than a social document, and then the claim is made that the text does not really say what it says. In other words, a text is a mere cover for some social, political reality. The mission of the critic is to uncover that reality. To read a text is to decipher it, stripping it of its supposed meanings to reach what the words conceal. Literary criticism becomes an exercise in investigating secrets, in the vein not so much of Sherlock Holmes as of Torquemada and State Prosecutor Vishinsky.

Shakespeare's *Tempest* turns into a fireworks display whose bright play of light blinds us to the base reality: the birth of modern imperialism. Prospero is the European master and Caliban his colonial slave. The text is a tissue of lies; by unraveling it, the critic unmasks the author, who is the accomplice of tyranny and oppression. No one escapes the ridiculous verdicts of these judges in their robes and mortarboards.

This change has affected the art not of writing poems but of reading them. Reading the *Odyssey* as a literary text is not the same as reading it as a social document. If we read it as an amazing adventure in which heroes are moved by strong, simple passions, the whole told with consummate verbal art at once noble and direct, how can we fail to be fascinated by the cunning of Ulysses as he tricks Polyphemus or unties the bonds of love with which Circe attempts to imprison him? For anyone who reads this as a document, it is no more than a chapter in the history of human superstition. The Circe fable shedding light on belief in magic and its relation to sexuality; the story of Polyphemus read as an allegory of combat between a tribe of aborigines (the Cyclopes) and a handful of imperialist adventurers. Indeed, the *Odyssey* describes mores of unquestionable interest to the historian, but it is neither a historical account nor an ethnographic study: it is a poem, a verbal creation. Any reader who does not pause in awe at the beauty of certain strophes is a brutish boor. Nor should we approach this age-old poem as a sort of cross-word puzzle which, once solved, will reveal to us the reality of Homeric Greece: a superstition-ridden agricultural society made up of miserable peasants, violent warriors and thieves, and liar poets. That is to say, yet another variant of class society and its iniquities. Such an interpretation, despite its crudity and oversimplification, may not be altogether wrong. But to read a poem in this way is like studying botany by scrutinizing a Corot or Monet landscape.

Outside the closed precinct of universities, the poetic tradition has been exposed to a continuous and insidious erosion which, precisely because it is not intentional, is extremely difficult to stop. The assault is not the result of a deliberate choice on the part of critics, as in the case of the doctrinaires I have mentioned, but of the nihilism inherent in all mechanisms. The agent of erosion is not an idea but a process: The growth of the publishing industry, combined with the power of publicity, has turned what was once the interchange of ideas, values, tastes, and opinions into a modern market. The literary world, like the artistic, scientific, and philosophical ones, was always an exchange, a trade in goods both material and spiritual: books are objects, and at the same time they are ideas and aesthetic forms. A famous literary review, published in Paris a few years before the Second World War, was called *Commerce*. The title, if I am not mistaken, came from

Valéry. I imagine he was alluding, with a certain arrogance, to the exchange of extremely rare spiritual and aesthetic goods among a very select group of demanding connoisseurs. An idea characteristic of Valéry, and likewise one that betrays an artisan's view of intellectual and literary commerce. The transformation of the "commerce" of half a century ago into today's editorial industry has been yet another victory of the mass market over former practices.

The links in the assembly line of the literary market: the author produces consumer items (books) that the publisher manufactures and distributes to consumers (readers). A ceaseless assembly line that continually provides new products which by their very nature can never entirely satisfy the consumer's hunger. An invention of modern capitalism, reminiscent of Tantalus: more, ever more—and never enough. Charles Fourier believed that in the state of true civilization, which he called Harmony, a limited number of long-lasting objects of incomparable quality would be produced. But in our societies, every effort is made to produce the greatest number of objects of mediocre quality, short duration, and rapid consumption. I do not deny the advantages of a market economy. In the developed nations, it is the cause of an abundance without precedent in history (even though this abundance is very often misleading and superfluous: creating false needs and failing to address certain essential ones). But I note that as production and consumption increase, so does waste. The mountain of books accumulating in libraries and bookstores raises a worrisome question: What to do with the surplus?

The poetic tradition, as I have already said, is the result of the intersection of two axes, one spatial and the other temporal. The spatial is the diversity of publics in continual intercommunication; the temporal is the continuity through generations of poets and readers. Intercommunication enriches the tradition by bringing to it new blood and new eyes. Karl Marx kept company with Dante, and Stendhal with Byron, because people of different groups—some of them lovers of philosophy or the economic sciences, others of the novel or of history—communicated with one another. The custom still exists, but it is dying out. One of my most pleasant literary memories is of an evening gathering in the home of the physicist Steven Weinberg, during which the conversation shifted spontaneously from elementary particles to the poetry of Donne and Marvell. This plurality of readers of different disciplines, brought together by similar tastes and values, is what is meant by a tradition. It does not matter that within that tradition opinions vary or are even opposite: we all read Goethe, but each of us reads him with different eyes.

In a past that is still recent, tradition was nourished by the Greco-Latin classics. Today they are much less widely read, though fortunately they have not disappeared entirely; translations of Homer, Virgil, Theocritus, and Horace are still done into a great number of the world's languages. On the other hand, we read modern writers in other languages far more frequently today than our fathers did. This network of coincidences and oppositions, some of them implicit, others explicit, constitutes the literary conversation of a period—a conversation almost always silent, conducted alone in a room with a book. As we read, we converse with authors in our own language and in other languages; some of those authors are alive, but the majority are not. Quevedo says, in a sonnet that seems to be written not on a sheet of paper but on a block of time that has turned to stone:

> *Retired to the peace of this desert,*
> *with a collection of books that are few but wise,*
> *I live in conversation with the departed*
> *and listen to the dead with my eyes.**

The contemporary publishing industry is dissolving the diversity of publics into one impersonal majority. This is not the result of a deliberate choice made by this person or that, nor is it the work of a conspiracy: the trend comes from the very nature of the system that rules the world of publishing. The literary trade today is motivated by purely economic considerations. The value of a book, thus, is the

---

*Quevedo wrote this sonnet in a little village in the north of the Sierra Morena, where he had a country house. *Desert* here means a place where there are few people.

number of people who purchase it. Earning money is a legitimate activity, and so is producing books for the "mass public"; but a literature dies and a society becomes decadent when the principal aim of publishers is to manufacture best-sellers and works for popular entertainment and consumption. There are indeed times when the popularity of a book and its excellence coincide: the works of Dickens and Balzac, Byron and Victor Hugo, to cite a few examples from the last century. But one should not close one's eyes to the fact that the history of literature in the West, especially in the Modern Age, has been and is that of minorities: writers and critics who rebelled against the status quo, poets and novelists who invented new forms, artists who were hermetic and difficult. The logic of the marketplace is not the logic of literature.

As the publishing industry becomes more and more impersonal—the field has now been invaded by powerful multinational corporations—economic considerations replace literary ones. All is not lost, of course: a handful of publishing houses, long established and venerable, have held out; small presses, set up to bring out books of poems in particular, turn up here and there; and finally, university presses in certain countries are beginning to replace commercial houses as publishers of works hard to sell. As to this last development, I have my doubts: the great literature of the nineteenth and twentieth centuries was written and printed, almost entirely, outside the universities. But apart from these laudable exceptions, the publishing industry, as it increases the number of editions put out and copies sold, tends to diminish the diversity of books and, as a consequence, the diversity of readers. In other sectors of the economy, a variety of merchandise is essential but the trend here is toward uniformity. The ideal is one and only one public: readers who all have exactly the same taste, who all read the same book. That book is many books: a new book by a different author may be published every day, but they are all really the same book.

The trend toward uniformity and a limited choice of books also affects the author. In the past, he wrote for a public, but at the same time for a reader who was a conversational partner. All poets dream of an ideal reader: his own, her own. Today the author must confront the publisher and his cohort of marketing executives. Moreover, in each house, especially in the United States, there are "editors" whose job it is to correct and adapt manuscripts. Certain editing practices, in and of themselves, are reasonable and justified, but as a whole they are deplorable: they threaten to destroy the diversity of authors, works, and readers. An incalculable loss, for not only are conversational partners lost, even though the number of readers increases, but the very notion of the conversational partner disappears. And along with it, the dialogue between author and reader. The most serious question of all: *From where* does a person write and read? For the modern publishing system, aided by advertising and television, all places, no matter how remote, are *here*. And where is here? In that nowhere that is everywhere. *Here* is situated in time; it is *right now*. The spatial axis dissolves into the temporal axis.

Marketing practices have an equally corrosive effect on the temporal axis of poetic tradition. The preeminence of the *now* weakens the ties that join us to the past. The press, television, and advertising offer us daily images of what is happening this minute in Patagonia, in Siberia, and in the neighborhood right next to ours. We are immersed in a now that never stops blinking and that gives us the feeling of constant acceleration. But are we really going somewhere? Or are we simply turning around and around in the same place? Whether illusory or real, the past whirls away at a dizzying pace and vanishes. The loss of the past inevitably results in the loss of the future. Since the eighteenth century, our civilization has been oriented toward the future. Its guide on this journey was the idea of progress, our polar star. For some years now, this star has been growing dimmer, and the present has been inheriting its brightness. But our present is a weightless thing: it floats along, it does not rise, it moves but makes no headway. It thinks it is going everywhere but is going nowhere: it has lost its sense of direction. The ends evaporate, and in compensation the means increase. Our present is a time that has no north to guide it. The expansion of the present, in the domain of literary tradition, manifests itself in the trend toward instantaneous communication. Endurance, that attribute of perfection, yields its place to quick consumption. The past and future vanish, and the present intensifies into a single instant: the three times are exhaled in one breath. The instant explodes and dissipates.

Poets have been the memory of their peoples. Homer sang of the deeds of a heroic age and told of what took place many years before: For him, the future did not exist; he lived in a static society whose eyes were focused on a past that was the model and source of the present. Later, the Greek poets were inspired by Homer, the Romans by the Greeks, Catullus followed the Alexandrians, Virgil guided Dante in his wanderings through Hell, Petrarch was the model for European poets, and so on down to our own day. Each poet is an undulation on the river of tradition, a moment of language. At times poets deny their tradition, but deny it only to invent another. The phenomenon is periodic, and has intensified in the modern era. From Romanticism to Surrealism, each poetic movement re-created its tradition. The Surrealists made lists of poets that were a parody both of the Last Judgment and of the final examination for a bachelor's degree. Each poet on the list was given a grade alongside his name: Baudelaire 8, Rimbaud 9½, Lautréamont 10 (summa cum laude), Apollinaire 7, Claudel −5, Valéry 1, Apuleius 6, Virgil 0, Dante 8, Sade 10 (with honors), and so on. Most poets choose their ancestors: Eliot chose the Metaphysical Poets and Laforgue;

Pound chose Cavalcanti and Li Po; Neruda chose Whitman; Borges chose another Whitman, not Neruda's; and Whitman chose an anonymous poet named Walt, a cosmos, and a borough of New York City. The invention of the past is a projection into the future. Every poet wishes to be read in the future, and in a profounder and more generous way than in his own time. It is not a thirst for fame; it is a thirst for life. The poet knows that he is simply a link in a chain, a bridge between yesterday and tomorrow. But suddenly, as this century draws to an end, he discovers that the bridge is suspended between two abysses: the past that is retreating in the distance, and the future that is crumbling. The poet feels lost in time.

Poetic forms are essential in poetry, because they are our recourse against death and the attrition of the years. Form is made to last. At times it is a challenge, at times a fortress or a monument, but it always represents the will to endure. Time concentrated and transmuted. It sets in opposition to real time not fixed structure but living architecture. Sonnet or ballad, Italian hendecasyllable or Japanese tanka, free verse or poem in prose—all forms and all meters are arks for crossing the sea of years and centuries. The memory of mankind. Art is a will to form because it is a will to endure. When a form becomes outworn or turns into a mere formula, the poet must invent another. Or find an old one and remake it: reinvent it. The invention of a form is often a new thing that is two or three hundred years old. There is nothing newer than the Chinese poems that Pound re-created, the songs in which Apollinaire brought medieval meters back to life, or the hesitant music, evasive yet evocative, that Darío learned from Verlaine, and Verlaine from Villon. But the publishing industry prefers digestible novelties to authentic novelties, formulas to forms.

The first half of this century was a period of invention and creation in all the arts. Thus it was also a time when new art was unpopular, as had been the case with Symbolism. Fortunately, poets and artists enjoyed the support of a number of patrons, publishers, art galleries, and collectors. The modern art that today hundreds of thousands admire in museums, and the books that everybody talks about and buys, were the art and literature of a small minority little more than fifty years ago. Since the Second World War, artistic activities have multiplied: museums, galleries, biennials, international auctions, rivers of gold, oceans of publicity. The same thing has occurred, though on a far lesser scale, in the world of publishing. Still, stereotypes predominate in both the visual arts and literature. The "in" word *postmodernism* designates an eclecticism. Rehashing abounds in painting and the other arts. It will be said that I exaggerate. Perhaps, but it is necessary to exaggerate. Although the causes of this situation are many and complex, I firmly believe that the principal cause is the transformation of what was once the literary and artistic trade into a modern financial market. An economic change that coincides with another, a moral-political change, in the democracies of the West: the turning of citizens into consumers.

A Balance Sheet
and a Prediction

My description of the state of poetry at the end of the century is incomplete, scarcely more than a sketch, a rough outline. But I would like to think that I have shown both the obstacles that stand in the way of its dissemination and the resources available to it in order to survive. No, poetry is not in the throes of death. It gives the impression that it is tired, or even suffering from a certain sterility; and, true, for the first time since the Romantic era, no poetic movement of major scope has appeared in thirty years. But the same can be said of the other arts. This phenomenon has not prevented the appearance of good poets and artists: every generation produces its own. The absence of poetic movements is a reflection of a great change our era has experienced: the twilight of the tradition of the sudden break. That twilight is one of the signs that presage either the end of modernity or its transformation. Certain people ask themselves: Are there still great poets, as there were just thirty years ago? This question comes from an error in perspective, because every generation makes the same complaint: Darío's contemporaries nostalgically longed for Bécquer, Bécquer's for Espronceda, Espronceda's for Meléndez Valdés. The phenomenon is cyclical and universal, characteristic of all times and all languages. Is poetry, is literature dying? No; we are living in a period of profound intellectual and spiritual malaise that coincides with a tremendous historical shock. An era is ending. Is another being born, or is what we are seeing and experiencing yet another metamorphosis of the Modern Age? Be it birth or rebirth, the sign of this end of the century is a question mark. But all times of uncertainty have been rich in poetic and artistic creations. I am not worried about the health of poetry, but about its place in the society we live in.

The arts most damaged from absorption by the financial market are precisely those that to all appearances have benefited the most. Painting and the novel are now consumer products. How can one form an opinion on all these changes? On one hand, the introduction of profitability as a criterion into a domain ruled by different values has debased the arts; but on the other, artistic production has been stimulated. The general mediocrity does not matter: in the long run, excellence always stands out and prevails. As for poetry, it has survived, even though condemned to hide in catacombs. In short, the situation is arduous and difficult—when has it not been?—but not desperate.

Having discussed the negative influences at some length, I feel it my duty now to point out the positive signs; though few in number, they are not to be dismissed. I already alluded to some of them but have not mentioned others, perhaps the most promising. Let me briefly touch on all of them. On the periphery of the major publishing market, small houses specializing in books of poems have sprung up in many places. There is intense activity in the area of translation, and the number of reviews devoted exclusively to poetry has greatly increased. There is an international brotherhood of aficionados of poetry, and these groups communicate with each other across linguistic and political boundaries. There are any number of international poetry festivals. Public poetry readings are a custom that steadily continues to spread and has been extended to radio and television (particularly in the United States and Great Britain). So it would not be rash to assume that there is a considerable though widely scattered public of readers, and that it grows from year to year. In the West, poets still do not have the social influence that the great Romantics had; but in Latin America and other places the poet is a public figure. In the Soviet Union, China, and all of Central Europe, poets have been eminent and at times central players in the struggle for democracy and against the Communist bureaucracies that hold the reins of power there.

In 1988 the Philip Morris Company, according to Donald Hall, commissioned the pollster Lou Harris to conduct a survey of "the arts and Americans." The National Center of the Arts published Harris's statistics shortly thereafter. A few figures: 97 million U.S. residents visit art museums at least once a year, and 60 million attend ballet and modern dance performances. How many photographers are there in the United States? Ninety million. And how many devotees study and practice ballet and dance? Forty million. After numbers such as these, it is not hard to believe that 42 million people in the United States write poems and stories. Nor is this liking for poetry and short stories—and the short-story genre lies somewhere between the prose poem and narrative—limited to the United States. We all know that here, too, a great number of people write poems, even though few manage to get them published. Since these enthusiasts are potential readers, what is surprising is not the fact that there are 42 million secret authors, but that so few of them buy and read books of poems. How does one explain this? The private author's envy of the public author? I do not believe so. I will propose a rough answer: Amateur authors cannot become active readers because they lack sufficient information about current literary developments and new poetic forms. With extremely few exceptions, their taste is that of the previous generation. This accounts for their triteness, and for the outdated form of what they write. Motivated by a legitimate but vague desire for self-expression, the amateur lacks that store of knowledge that comes from the frequent reading of good poetry. This knowledge is not only theoretical; it is also experience, which becomes second nature. It is, in other words, the *knowledge of how to go about writing*. Who is to blame for this situation? In part, the publishers, and those responsible for the current system of education.

Publishers have ignored these potential readers, these enthusiasts who write poems. Which is not surprising: almost all publishers belong to the ruling technocracies and therefore worship the dubious social sciences, scorn the classics, and mistrust poetry, considering it a fruitless activity or an archaic pastime. For this reason, what must be done, to begin with, is educate publishers, their assistants, and their spokesmen. An extremely difficult task, but not an impossible one. It may not be feasible or even desirable to change this gigantic industry, but surely it is possible to create small autonomous units whose purpose is to produce books that satisfy the needs of minorities. In other words, we need someone to take the risk of betting on the plurality of spiritual and aesthetic tastes, enthusiasms, and interests. The case of the American publishing house New Directions is a notable example. James Laughlin, the son of a well-to-do family, studied at Harvard some fifty years ago. A poetry lover despite his disappointment at the professors he had, he decided to spend some time in Rapallo, where Ezra Pound was the focal point of a small group devoted to the study of poetry—the "Ezraversity," as Pound himself called his circle. After six months of sharing their experiences, Pound and Laughlin made a pact: Laughlin would become a publisher and devote himself to bringing out books by Pound, William Carlos Williams, and other poets of that time. Thus New Directions came into being. It is a house that has now lasted more than half a century and accomplished two equally difficult things: refusing to become a gigantic multinational corporation, while publishing not only many valuable North American poets but also the corpus of modern European and Latin American poetry.

In his recent volume of delightful and intelligent prose (*Recollections of a Publisher,* 1989), Laughlin notes that Pound recommended what books he should publish but gave him no advice about how to sell them. He adds: "Perhaps he didn't know or didn't care. I can't remember his exact phrase but he seemed quite content if something he had written and given to some obscure magazine reached the eyes and beans of twenty-seven readers, if they were the right readers, the ones who would diffuse his ideas." Pound was quite right: a book's worth becomes known not by way of loudspeakers advertising it, but by word of mouth and sotto voce. Laughlin had the good sense not to follow all of Pound's advice: he did not publish, for instance, the eccentric economic theories of Major Clifford Hugh Douglas. But he quickly understood that the new literature, unanimously scorned by university professors and well-entrenched critics, could win a small but fervent public. It was an undertaking that went against current tastes and deliberately appealed to a minority. In a letter, Pound wrote to his young friend: "For Christ's sake meditate on something I once told you: Nothing written for pay is worth anything; only what has been written *against* the market. There is nothing so inebriating as earning money. Big check and you think you have *done* something and two years later there is nothing bloody well to show for it." These lines were written in 1940. Nine years later, Pound renewed the charge: "The death of all the old staid American publishing houses would be a sign of God's favor to humanity. There are no known acts on the part of these firms that ever favored living writers or literature."

The function of small independent publishing houses can be compared to the creation of antibodies to defend an organism. Surrounded by general indifference, a group of talented young people get together and decide to found a review. One of them proves to be a brave and clever captain, capable of setting up camp in philistine territory. In a short time, the review becomes an influential publishing house and its books transform the public's taste and ideas. I am speaking here of the *Nouvelle Revue Française,* founded by André Gide and Gaston Gallimard. Or the review may be founded around a great and highly esteemed personality: the *Revista de Occidente* and José Ortega y Gasset. The intellectual stimulus of this review, its books, and Ortega y Gasset's own body of work was enormous and profound for my generation. When I was twenty, among the *Revista de Occidente* books that reached my hands were Guillén's *Cántico,* García Lorca's *Romancero gitano,* and Alberti's *Cal y canto.* Shortly thereafter, José Bergamín's *Cruz y Raya* published notable works, and one of them astounded all of us: Neruda's *Residencia en la tierra.* In those same years there appeared in Buenos Aires the review *Sur,* the prime mover of which was Victoria Ocampo, aided by a modest and subtle talent: José Bianco. *Sur* also published books: under its imprint appeared, among others, Borges's *The Garden of Forking Paths.* Sometimes miners leave the bowels of the earth, rise to the surface, enter the corridors of the fortresses of publishing, and become the advisers and inspirers of the princes of the industry—like Eliot in his office at Faber and Faber in London.

It would be tiresome to give more examples, but it is worth adding that two features distinguish such endeavors. The first: the birth of a small publishing enterprise results from the joint action of a group of writers, most often young ones. This group senses, not always clearly, that it has something new or different to say. The review or publishing house gives expression to the novelty not so much of a generation as of a sensibility, a language, or a vision. If there is nothing new to say, the house fails or turns into a business. The second feature: the review's publications express the tastes and ideas of a minority; thus they are directed against reigning tastes and ideas. These two features define the phenomenon: it is a break with the old order and the incursion of a new literature. Both the break and the incursion are relative: each break confirms tradition and continues it; each innovation is nurtured by the innovations of the past; each rupture is an homage to those who have gone before.

This twofold movement of negation and affirmation, of rupture and filial attachment, is constant in the history of all literatures and most particularly modern literature. Its absence in the literary life of our day is a worrisome sign. In the Modern Age, the activity of minorities has been the breath of life of literary tradition. The disappearance of minorities and their means of expression—reviews and small publishing houses—in favor of uniformity would mean not only a mutilation of the living body of literature, but also, perhaps, its death. There would no longer be literature, only best-sellers. I am afraid that this is the ideal of a fair number of publishers. Let us hope that their dream never comes true. But it is true that we are living through a period of uncertainty in the realm of all the arts. Something is definitely missing in contemporary literature. That something is the word *no,* a word that has always been the forerunner of great affirmations. But I am sure that *something,* hidden in the folds of this century now drawing to a close, is brewing.

The education of publishers is necessary to preserve literary tradition, a tradition that is the dual activity of minorities and majorities, ruptures and repetitions. The education of academics is also necessary. I have already mentioned the harmful effects of the modern tendency to consider literary works as historical and social documents. This intellectual vogue is due not to the inveterate pedantry of scholars, though pedantry does enter the picture, but to the intellectual fascination that orthodoxies have always exercised. To certain minds there is nothing more attractive than "universal compendiums and general explanations of the world," as Marx said. He was referring to religion, little knowing that he was prophesying the fate of his own doctrine in the twentieth century. But this is not the first time in history that poetry has been the object of deformations and mutilations imposed by the geometrical absolutism of an orthodoxy. The great anthology attributed to Confucius *(Shih Ching)* contains many love poems that not infrequently call to mind the traditional erotic lyric poetry of Spain. But the prudishness of the mandarins transformed those poems, poems that sing of capricious and unusual passion, into rigid political allegories and moralizing fables. In the place of the bonds of passion that unite or estrange lovers, the official interpretation imposed the geometry of the code that governs the relations between the ruler and his ministers. In our civilization, other orthodoxies, the Jewish and the Christian, turned poems known to be erotic, such as the *Song of Songs,* into a religious allegory of the love of Jehovah for Israel or of Christ for his Church. The negation of the body, made more severe by the influence of Platonism on Christian philosophy, led the great Menéndez Pelayo to lament the forwardness of Saint Teresa of Avila, who used popular love songs to celebrate the nuptials of the soul with God. On the other side of the English Channel, a similar sense of scandal was voiced: shortly before his death, Auden deplored the excessive sensuality of certain verses of Saint John of the Cross.

The censure of religious orthodoxies is even so less ridiculous than certain scientistic interpretations. I am thinking now not of sociology but of psychoanalysis. Some professors are determined to see in Saint John of the Cross's "Spiritual Canticle" a poem of profane love, and in his "Dark Night" the adventure of a young girl who steals from her house to meet her beau in a clearing in the woods. Reading these poems as texts about profane love—or as sublimations of sexual, perhaps homoerotic, tendencies—is the equivalent of the political reading to which Chinese scholars subjected the *Shih Ching*. Such interpretation is naive and oversimplified: it ignores the ambiguity of these poems, their continual movement back and forth between the sacred and the profane, the spiritual and the sensual, the intellectual and the carnal. Nor is this ambiguity limited to Saint John of the Cross; it appears in all the great texts of the mystics, be they Christians or Muslims, Hindus or Taoists. Only among the Neoplatonists, as E. R. Dodds points out, was a sharp line drawn between the body and the soul (and not by all of them). Tantrism in the East and various Gnostic sects in the West are the purest and most extreme examples of the ancient and irrepressible tendency to commingle sensation and idea, act and symbol.

The confusion between the religious and the erotic is a constant feature of profane poetry, too. Dante and Donne, Quevedo and Baudelaire, Lope de Vega and Sor Juana, Petrarch and Ronsard, Novalis and Blake, not to mention lesser poets like Medrana and López Velarde, continually employ religious terms to describe experiences of sensual passion. The fact that Saint John of the Cross resorts to erotic images, many of which come from learned poetry or popular songs, is perfectly natural. But Saint John of the Cross proves rather timid, when we turn to the Sufi poets or Tantric texts. In the Tantric texts, for example, the term *sukra* (semen) is also used to refer to sudden enlightenment *(bodhicitta);* and orgasm and spiritual ecstasy are not distinguished, both are called *mahasukka* (great bliss). If there is no greater bliss than satisfied human love, and no worse misfortune than love denied, why not compare it to mystical love? Both are expressions of the same vital force.

This brief digression has served, at least, to explain what I meant when I spoke of educating the learned. I do not disdain their store of knowledge, which is extensive and diverse, but they must learn all over again to read a poem as a poetic text and not as some social or psychoanalytic document.*

I am severe in my judgment of academics because the continuity of the poetic tradition depends, in large part, on them. Had it not been for Greek tutors, no one would have recited the Homeric poems, and Greece would not have been Greece. And I grant that the poetic tradition endures, even though ill treated, thanks to them; unlike the classics, our national poetic tradition is still taught and cultivated in almost every university. The fondness of young people for poetry and the vitality of this public in the United States results from the attention paid by universities to the teaching of the poetic tradition of the language. In certain countries, such as England, Russia, Germany, and Japan, love of the national poetic tradition is a venerable custom and still intact: Shakespeare continues to be a god to the English, Goethe to the Germans, and Pushkin to the Russians. In Latin America, this tradition is dying out; in certain countries it has disappeared altogether. But we are dealing with

---

*An example of this good sort of reading is Domingo Yndurain's excellent edition of the poetic works of Saint John of the Cross, published under the title *Poesías* (Madrid: Cátedra, 1983).

a sick continent. In no other part of the world has the loss of historical memory been as widespread, as profound, and as devastating in its consequences as in our countries.

I must add that the attitude of universities toward poets has varied a great deal, particularly in the United States, where the universities are the best and the wealthiest. In the past, poets from a university milieu could be counted on one's fingers. But after the Second World War, universities in the United States opened their doors to them; poets were invited not only to read their poems but to occupy academic chairs and conduct seminars. I look upon this change with mixed feelings. The poet, so often regarded by the middle class and academic institutions as a pariah and an idler, has been given a place of honor; at the same time, the sedentary life of the university, basically intellectual and still bookish, and on the sidelines of city life, can narrow a poet's vision. The experience of the poet must be direct, vast, and varied: it did Eliot no harm to work in a bank or Neruda to be a consul in Rangoon. But a few of the best contemporary poets of the United States, such as Robert Lowell and Elizabeth Bishop, did survive undamaged their passage through the aseptic paradise of academia, perhaps because they found in those cloisters a momentary respite from the chaos of their lives. Another innovation: "poetry workshops," in which a poet teaches his craft to a group of students. Such workshops have been set up in almost all universities in the United States (and in

Mexico as well). I am of the opinion that they have done more harm than good. If we wish to "teach how to write," perhaps we should return to the venerable tradition of classes in composition, rhetoric, and the study of classical models.

As in the Middle Ages, poets are taking refuge in universities, but it would be most unfortunate if they were to abandon city life. Villon was a son of the university, but his life as a poet was created (and destroyed) by the streets of Paris. The poetry that Villon exemplifies satisfies emotional and spiritual needs that are at once personal and communal. Some of his poems are profound, and others merely merge with the flow of daily existence: love affairs, sorrows, regrets, visions, the whole range. Poetry sings of what is happening; its function is to give form to everyday life and make it visible. I do not claim that this is its only mission, although it is the oldest, most permanent, and most universal one. While not all peoples have a *Divine Comedy* or a *Paradise Lost,* they all have a poetic tradition—songs, ballads, narrative verse—that becomes one with their history itself. In all times and places, songs and tales in verse have been composed—of love or duels, of loneliness or communal celebration. These stanzas have been sung in places of worship and in public squares, in salons and in taverns, in theaters and in boudoirs. The tradition is still alive, as demonstrated by the tremendous fame that surrounds popular composers, musicians, and singers. Television, radio, and phonograph records endlessly reproduce their compositions, voices, and images. Poetic and musical forms may have changed, but the subjects of a John Lennon are not all that different from those of the narrative verses and songs of the sixteenth and seventeenth centuries. And the quality? As in the shops, there is a little of everything: what is good is always rare. But these songs, whatever their merit, satisfy a psychological need felt as keenly today as it was three centuries ago. Or more precisely, as it was thousands of years ago.

As I touch on this subject, I again come across an absence. Among widely known contemporary poets, very few have shown interest in cultivating the traditional genres. This represents a great loss. Traditional poems and songs are our liveliest and purest poetic heritage. It is a tradition that exists in all languages and that in our own is particularly rich. It is born with the language, it produces the sprawling anthology of ballads and narrative verse we call the *Romancero,* it crosses the sea and spreads throughout the continent wherever Spanish is spoken and read. Many of these poems are anonymous, and others are the work of our most lofty poets, an admirable fusion of the collective and the individual. The renaissance of poetry in Spanish in the first third of the twentieth century was due in large part to the influence of traditional lyric poetry, preserved and purified by Bécquer, and later on by Juan Ramón Jiménez and Antonio and Manuel Machado. In this hemisphere, we had neither a García Lorca nor an Alberti, but we did have a brief, bright flash of Afro-American poetry. But no matter how attractive the forms of traditional songs and ballads may be, popular contemporary poetry has no reason to follow these models formally. Poets must search for forms and rhythms more in harmony with the language and the life of our cities. An example of a body of poetry that retrieves the spirit of tradition but not its forms is the work of Jacques Prévert, a Surrealist. But the instances I have mentioned—to which Brecht may be added—are isolated cases. Perhaps tomorrow's poets will decide to explore this vast territory, the soul of a people.

No doubt some of my readers will raise an eyebrow in surprise, that in speaking of poetry in the public life of the city I failed to mention "committed poets." Political poetry was of major importance in the first half of the twentieth century, but very few of the poems written in those years attained the universality of genuine poetry. Its authors were too close to news bulletins and much too far away from the events themselves. The news bulletin turns into mere propaganda, whereas the event itself is history suddenly making an appearance. Ours is a puzzling reality, and we must decipher it if we are not to be devoured. History devoured the so-called *poètes engagés*. They believed in justice and in the emancipation of humanity, but theirs was a blind faith, and they mistook oppressors for tyrants. What they lacked was penetration—or, better put, vision. For this reason their poems have aged badly in less than thirty years. The political history of the twentieth century, with its two complementary facets, socialist realism and commitment, dramatizes one of the most peculiar phenomena of our time: the fascination of many artists and intellectuals for authoritarian regimes. The mystery of "totalitarian seduction," as Jean-François Revel calls it, is psychological and historical; it belongs to the study of ethical aberrations and mass deliriums. It may well be that two elements were decisive: the passion for the Absolute and the idolatry of power. The Idea and Caesar. A great deal has been written on the subject, yet the puzzle has by no means been solved.

I have alluded more than once in these pages to the lack of popularity of the new poetry, followed years later by its public consecration. With a sort of astronomical regularity, in which it is not unreasonable to see the mysterious workings of the "poetic justice" of antiquity, the poets of the Modern Age begin their careers in obscurity; later they are the target of satires and the butt of jokes; and finally, invariably, they end up being beatified in public ceremonies. Often the recognition takes place post mortem. But not always: Eliot, Neruda, and Valéry became living myths. Even in his own time, Baudelaire drew attention to the cyclical nature of the phenomenon, and in his *Advice to Young Littérateurs,* which the new poets of 1990 could well read with profit, he writes:

As for those who devote themselves to poetry with talent, I advise them never to abandon it. Poetry is one of the arts that brings the best return, but it is a type of investment that produces no interest until later—though at a very high rate, I might add. I challenge those who are envious to point out to me good verses that have ruined a publisher.

I have spoken of the publishing market but not of the new means of communication. I have no desire to rehash the arguments about what has been called the nihilism of technology or the relation between technology and poetry. Having devoted a number of essays to the subject,* I will not repeat them, but confine myself to saying that in them I attempted to show the fundamental opposition that exists between modern technology and poetry. Technology is not an image of the world but a praxis, an action whose purpose is to change it and to some extent cast it aside;

---

*The oldest of these is *Los signos en rotación,* published first as a slim separate volume along the lines of a "poetic manifesto" (*Sur,* 1965) and later included in the second and definitive edition of *El arco y la lira* (1967), in which it appears as the final chapter. Another essay is "La nueva analogía: Poesía y Tecnología" (1967), reprinted as "La modernidad y sus desenlaces" in the first part of *El signo y el garabato* (1973). Another is "El pacto verbal" (1980), included in *Hombres en su siglo* (1984) and which appears in *Convergences: Essays on Art and Literature,* tr. Helen Lane (New York: Harcourt Brace Jovanovich, 1987).

poetry, on the other hand, has always been a vision of the world. I pointed out, however, that poetry is already making use of the new means of communication, and I advised poets to use them more boldly and imaginatively. Poetry has existed side by side with all societies and has used all the means of communication that those societies have placed at its disposal, from tortoise and conch shells to the most sophisticated musical intruments, from an inscription on a brick to a manuscript illuminated in vermilion, from a book to a phonograph record and magnetic tape.

As often happens, my first reflections on the subject coincided with my own poetic endeavors: visual poetry, texts that moved, and the publishing of a poem, "Blanco," in which I tried to combine in an unusual way the two axes of the writing and the reading of poems: the spatial and the temporal.* In the case of "Blanco," I set myself the task of designing a book whose pages and typography were the physical projection of a mental experience: the reading of a poem that unfolds both in space and time. My research led to the recognition of unsuspected and unexplored possibilities in the filmstrip and the television screen. Both are

---

*"Blanco" (1966): *Discos visuales* (1968); *Topoemas* (1968); *Anotaciones/Rotaciones* (1974). *Discos visuales* was made in collaboration with Vicente Rojo, and *Anotaciones/Rotaciones* with Toshihiro Katayama. There is an English translation, by Eliot Weinberger, of "Blanco": published by The Press in New York (limited edition, with graphic designs by Toshihiro Katayama).

the equivalent of a page of a book. An entirely separate page, as Mallarmé wished, but at the same time possessing an attribute he never dreamed of: movement. A moving page, in which a moving text appears. A space that elapses: time.

In the beginning, poetry was oral: an ascending column made of verses. Rhythmical verbal unities that appeared and disappeared, one after the other, in the air. Góngora likens poetic discourse to the current of a river. But a river runs between two banks, whereas the verbal stream of a poem flows through and disappears into the air. It is time in its purest form. Later, poetry relied on writing; ever since, it has made use of the written sign and spoken word. The two traditions developed along parallel lines, although they have constantly crossed and intermingled. In certain countries and periods, written poetry added a visual element to graphic signs: Chinese, Japanese, Arabic, and Persian calligraphy; illuminated manuscripts; books and poems illustrated by great artists; unusual typographies. One of the most transcendent moments of this tradition in the modern era was Mallarmé's *Un coup de dés.* In this poem, the visual composition is ruled by a prosody different from metrical verse: a subtle play between the typography and the recital of the poem. But an internal recital: words spoken and heard with the eyes and the mind.

In all written forms of poetry, the graphic sign acts as a function of the oral sign. However expressive or refined the calligraphy of a Chinese poem may be, the reader *hears mentally,* behind the elegant or energetic character, the words of the text, their verbal music. The calligraphed page is a tissue of brush strokes that denote sounds and meanings. The same thing occurs with the typographical composition of *Un coup de dés*. For that reason Mallarmé, in the prologue of his poem, says: "The retreats, advances, prolongations, and fugues of the poem, and its very layout, become a musical score for anyone who cares to read it aloud." Even in Apollinaire's calligrams, which are more purely visual, the spoken word, the sound element, underpins the designed and written text. One of the weaknesses of Surrealism was its scorn for prosody. An indifference belied, moreover, by the poetic practice itself of the Surrealist poets: their texts abound in wordplay and clashes between sound and sense. In no other literary genre is the union between sound and sense as intimate as in poetry. This is what distinguishes a poem from other literary forms—this is its essential characteristic. The poem is a rhythmical verbal organism, an object made of words said and heard, not words written or read.

We are now in a position to understand the real significance of public poetry readings. It is one of the positive signs that I mentioned previously. A return to the origin of poetry, a return to the source. And for that very reason the possibilities of the television screen are immense. First of all, the increasing popularity of videocassettes frees us from the tyranny of ratings and clears the way for a plurality of publics. Second, on the television screen the two great poetic traditions, the written and the spoken, come together. The screen is a page that favors the design of compositions even more complex than those envisioned by Mallarmé. Letters can appear in different colors, and in motion. The page thus becomes a surface that breathes, elapses, and changes from color to color. And the human voice, many voices, can be combined with the letters. Finally, the visual images and the sound elements, instead of serving as mere decoration, can become organic parts of the body of the poem.

Some of us, in different cities, independently of each other, have begun to use the television screen to project our poems. The difficulties are tremendous—I for my part confess that I am feeling my way—but the opportunities that are opening up little by little are equally tremendous. I am certain that poems projected on the TV screen are destined to become a new poetic form. This genre will affect the dissemination and reception of poetry in a way no less profound than did, in its day, the printing press. And therefore it will bring about, finally, the union of the privileged senses of our species: sight and hearing, the image and the word. Very soon, I am convinced, television poetry will be able to satisfy the dual nature of aesthetic pleasure and the poetic experience: celebration and contemplation. The first is participation, communion; the second is a silent dialogue with the universe and with ourselves. In the poem of the future, heard and read, seen and listened to, the two will be joined. Celebration and contemplation: on the animated page of the screen, the typography will be a jetting fountain of signs, strokes, and images possessing color and movement; the voices, in turn, will draw a geometry of echoes and reflections, a fabric of interwoven air, sounds, and meanings.

The Other Voice

While writing these reflections, every so often I have re-called, not without sadness, the struggles that certain of us poets, writers, and artists have waged for many years and in different countries. In my youth, the struggle against "socialist realism," a doctrine that subjected literature to the dictates of a State and a Party that, in the name of the liberation of mankind, was erecting monuments to the whip and the boot. Later, the debate over "committed" literature. If Sartre's idea of *la littérature engagée* was con-fused, the interpretations it gave rise to, in Latin America in particular, were actually harmful. It was necessary to fumigate them through criticism. I do not regret those

battles; they were worthwhile. Today literature and the arts
are exposed to a different danger: they are threatened not
by a doctrine or a political party but by a faceless, soulless,
and directionless economic process. The market is circular,
impersonal, impartial, inflexible. Some will tell me that this
is as it should be. Perhaps. But the market, blind and deaf,
is not fond of literature or of risk, and it does not know
how to choose. Its censorship is not ideological: it has no
ideas. It knows all about prices but nothing about values.

It is impossible to fight, I know, against the market
economy, or to deny its benefits. But now that totalitarian
socialism, by all indications, is falling apart and has ceased
to be a threat to democratic societies, a new political and
social way of thinking may perhaps permit less onerous
forms of exchange. This is my ardent hope. Now that the
cruel utopias that bloodied our century have vanished, the
time has come at last to begin a radical, more human
reform of liberal capitalist society. And a reform, too, of the
peoples on the periphery, grouped together under the du-
bious title of the Third World. Perhaps these impoverished
nations—victims of a succession of archaic tyrannies and
astute demagogues, of rapacious oligarchies and delirious
intellectuals enamored of violence—severely chastised as
they have been by the disasters of recent decades, will find
their political salvation and, with it, a modicum of well-
being. No one in his right mind can think that the crisis
that today brings chaos to the countries that have lived

under the despotism of bureaucratic Communism will not spread to the rest of the world. We are living through a change of times: not a revolution but, in the long-standing and profoundest sense of the word, a revolt—a return to the origin, to the beginning. We are witnessing not the end of history, as a certain professor in the United States has claimed, but a rebeginning. The resurrection of buried realities, the reappearance of what was forgotten and repressed, which can lead, as it has at other times in history, to regeneration. Returns to the origin are almost always revolts: renovations, renaissances.*

In the second half of the eighteenth century there appeared a complex and powerful current of ideas, sentiments, aspirations, and dreams (some lucid, some insane) that crystallized in the French and American revolutions. Our history, the history of our time, begins with them. The movement born of these two great revolutions runs through the twentieth century like a river that repeatedly goes underground and resurfaces. As it flows, it changes; as it changes, it ceaselessly returns to its source. Each resurfacing is accompanied by new ideas and hypotheses, utopias,

---

*See *Corriente alterna* (1967), part 3 in particular (*Alternating Current*, trans. Helen Lane [New York: Viking, 1973]); and *Tiempo Nublado* (1983), chapters 4 and 5 (*One Earth, Four or Five Worlds: Reflections on Contemporary History*, trans. Helen Lane [New York: Harcourt Brace Jovanovich, 1987]).

programs of social and political reform. The philosophies of the Enlightenment were modified; from the liberal thought of a Tocqueville or a John Stuart Mill sprouted new, nostalgic ideologies—of a better past, or (equally critical of the present) of a freer, more just and peaceful future. The utopias soon became revolutionary programs, often with scientific pretensions. The great aberration of the last century was to look to science for the foundation that the old philosophy had sought in reason or in divine revelation. Marxism, for instance, while it did not renounce the dialectic inherited from Hegel (an illusory logic), tried to take advantage of Ricardo's contributions to economic theory; later, and with even less justification, it tried to turn Darwin's theory of evolution to its own uses.

Anarchist and socialist doctrines were the great political and social ferment of the second half of the twentieth century. But in our century two major wars, followed by violent revolutions in Asia and one of the farthermost parts of Europe, interrupted the process of gradual change that many socialists and democrats had predicted. As for the totalitarianisms that arose from the Bolshevik version of Marxism, they were the backfire of socialism—yet another proof that the material basis of history was resistant to the pretensions of theory. Today we are witnessing the impressive refutation of so-called scientific socialism. Those who believe in scientific socialism must now admit that the regimes in question were never very socialist or very scientific. But does the discrediting of this terrible experiment also affect the libertarian, egalitarian aspirations that spurred on the anarchist and socialist thinkers of the last century? I do not believe so. Confronted with the iniquities of the capitalist system, these men asked themselves a number of questions. Questions that remain unanswered.

It is true that the capitalist system has shown a tremendous capacity for renewal: while increasing its efficiency many times over, it has reformed and humanized itself. Abundance reigns in the West, and a large, prosperous middle class now includes much of the old proletariat. But this prosperity reaches only a fraction of the human species. And who can deny the injustice and the inequality that still exist in the most developed nations? The many deplorable aspects of the consumer society? Abundance has not made Europeans or North Americans more kindhearted, or wiser, or happier. To measure our aesthetic impoverishment, our moral and spiritual baseness, we need only compare ourselves with an Athenian of the fifth century B.C., a Roman in the days of Trajan and Marcus Aurelius, or a fifteenth-century Florentine.

The programs of socialists and libertarian writers were often naive, simplistic, and sometimes brutal and despotic. But neither the deficiencies, lacunae, errors, and excesses of these programs nor their colossal historical failure invalidates the questions these people asked themselves. I am of the opinion that the time is coming for us to ask ourselves these same questions. Our answers, almost certainly, will be different; this is only natural. But they will be inspired by similar motives and must satisfy similar hopes. The questions are basic ones. They appear with the birth of the modern era, and in them lies, like a kernel, the entire history of our time, its chimeras and contradictions, its aberrations and illuminations. Without the risk of vastly oversimplifying them, they can be summarized by the three cardinal words of modern democracy: liberty, equality, fraternity. The relation between these is unclear—or, rather, problematical. They contain a mutual contradiction. Where is the bridge to link them?

As I see it, the central word of the triad is *fraternity*. The other two are intermeshed with it. Liberty can exist without equality, and equality without liberty. Liberty, in isolation, makes inequalities more profound and provokes tyrannies; equality oppresses liberty and in the end destroys it. But fraternity is the nexus that connects them, the virtue that humanizes and harmonizes them. Its other name is solidarity, a living heritage of Christianity, a modern version of the venerable word *charity*. Which was known to neither the Greeks nor the Romans, who were enamored of liberty but unaware of true compassion. Given the natural differences between human beings, equality is an ethical aspiration that cannot be realized without recourse either to despotism or to an act of fraternity. My liberty fatally comes face-to-face with the liberty of the other and seeks to destroy it. The one and only bridge that can reconcile these two brothers continually at sword's point with each other—a bridge made of interlinked arms—is fraternity. In the days to come, a new political philosophy could be founded on this humble, simple, evident truth. Only fraternity can dispel the circular nightmare of the market. Please note that I am not imagining or predicting this line of thought: it is the heir of the dual tradition of modernity—the liberal/socialist tradition. I do not believe it should be repeated; it should be transcended. That would be a real renewal.

In the light of these ideas, or rather, hopes, the question posed initially—Who reads books of poems?—takes on its true meaning. In the past, the readers of poems belonged to the ruling classes: Greek citizens, Roman patricians and *equites,* medieval clerics, courtiers of the Baroque age, intellectuals belonging to the bourgeoisie. In some cases these readers were actually rulers, great rulers like Pericles, Augustus, and Hadrian; or weak but sensitive like Philip IV ("our good king," as Manuel Machado calls him) and the unfortunate emperor Hsüan-t'ung; or enlightened despots like Frederick the Great. The big change takes place in the Modern Age: since the Romantic era, the readers of poems have been, like the poets themselves, loners and dissidents. Bourgeois poets and readers, but in rebellion against their background, their class, and the ethics of their world. This is one of the most incontrovertible glories of the bourgeoisie, the social class that took power with the weapon of critical thought and has never stopped using it to analyze itself and its works. The examination of conscience and the remorse that accompanies it, a legacy from Christianity, have been and are the most powerful remedy against the ills of our civilization.

In modernity's tradition of criticism and rebellion, poetry occupies a place at once central and eccentric. Central because, from the beginning, it was an essential part of the great current of criticism and subversion that ran through the nineteenth and twentieth centuries. Almost all our great poets have participated, at one time or another, in these movements of emancipation. But the uniqueness of modern poetry lies in its having been the expression of realities and dreams rooted more deeply in the past than in the intellectual geometries of the revolutionaries and the conceptual prisons of the utopians. At one of its extremes, poetry touches the electric border of religious vision. For this reason it has been alternately revolutionary and reactionary. It is not surprising, then, that all its loves have ended in divorce and its conversions in apostasy. Poetry, from its birth beneath the sudden lightning flash of Romanticism that destroyed the symmetries of the eighteenth century, down to the violent shadow cast by our own era, has continually been a stubborn, intractable heterodoxy. An incessant zigzagging rebellion against doctrines and churches. But at the same time, a no less constant love of humiliated reality, scorning the manipulations of fideism and speculations of rationalism. Poetry: the stone of scandal of modernity.

Between revolution and religion, poetry is the *other* voice. Its voice is *other* because it is the voice of the passions and of visions. It is otherworldly and this-worldly, of days long gone and of this very day, an antiquity without dates. Heretical and devout, innocent and perverted, limpid and murky, aerial and subterranean, of the hermitage and of the corner bar, within hand's reach and always beyond. All poets in the moments, long or short, of poetry, if they are really poets, hear the *other* voice. It is their own, someone else's, no one else's, no one's, and everyone's. Nothing distinguishes a poet from other men and women but those moments—rare yet frequent—in which, being themselves, they are other. The possession of strange forces and powers, the sudden emergence of a store of psychic knowledge buried in the most private depths of their being, or is it a singular ability to associate words, images, sounds, forms? It is not easy to answer such questions. But I do not believe that poetry is simply an *ability*. And even if it were, from where does it come? In sum, no matter what it may be, what is certain is that the great oddness of the poetic phenomenon suggests an ailment that still awaits a physician's diagnosis. Ancient medicine—and ancient philosophy, too, beginning with Plato—attributed the poetic faculty to a psychic disorder. A mania, in other words, a sacred fury, an enthusiasm, a transport. But mania is only one of the poles of the disorder; the other is *absentia,* inner emptiness, that "melancholy apathy" that the poet speaks of. Fullness and emptiness, flight and fall, enthusiasm and melancholy: poetry.

The oddness of the poet becomes more emphatic when we consider his social background. All modern poets, aside from a half-dozen aristocrats, have belonged to the middle class. They have all had a university education. Some were lawyers, journalists, doctors, professors, and diplomats, others were public relations and advertising executives, bankers, businessmen, important or unimportant bureaucrats. A few, such as Verlaine and Rimbaud, were parasites and fugitives from the law. But Verlaine had a small investment income, and Rimbaud was a dropout from the provincial bourgeoisie. They were all products of that great historical creation of modernity, the bourgeoisie. And for that very reason they were all, without exception, violent enemies of modernity. Enemies and victims. Hence—yet another paradox—they were fully modern. Heterodox when they bestowed their blessing on the established order, like Eliot, or when they crossed themselves, like Claudel, or when they recited Leninist litanies, like Brecht and Neruda; libertarian when they waved their censer to perfume a demagogue disguised as Caesar, like Pound. All of them, whether in uniform or in rags, female poets and male, poets of every sex and of none, of every profession, belief, party, and sect, poets wandering over the four corners of the earth and poets who never left their city, neighborhood, room: all of them heard, not outside but inside themselves (thunder, a rumbling in the intestines, a rush of water), the *other* voice. Never the voice of here and now, which is the modern voice, but the voice from beyond, the other one, the one of the beginning.

The singularity of modern poetry does not come from the ideas or the attitudes of the poet: it comes from his voice. That is, from the accent of his voice. It is an indefinable but unmistakable modulation that makes it *other*. The mark not of original sin but of original difference. The antimodern modernity of our poetry, torn between revolution and religion, hesitating between weeping like Heraclitus and laughing like Democritus, is a transgression. But a transgression that is almost always involuntary, without the poet's intention. It bursts forth, as I have said, from an original difference; it is not an addition or an artificial attachment like false teeth or a wig, but the very essence of poetry in the Modern Age. The reason for the singularity of poetry is historical. A poem may be modern because of its subject, language, and form, but because of its profound nature, its voice is antimodern, expressing realities that are not only far older than, but also impermeable to, the changes of history. Since the Paleolithic, poetry has been a part of the life of all human societies; no society exists that has not known one form of poetry or another. But although tied to a specific soil and a specific history, poetry has always been open, in each and every one of its manifestations, to a transhistorical beyond. I do not mean a religious beyond: I am speaking of the perception of the *other side* of reality. That perception is common to all men in all periods; it is an experience that seems to me to be *prior* to all religions and philosophies.

In a world ruled by the logic of the marketplace, or in Communist countries by state planning, poetry is an activity that brings no return whatsoever. Its products are scarcely salable and very nearly useless (except as propaganda in dictatorships and totalitarian ideocracies). To the modern mind, even though it will not admit this to itself, poetry is energy, time, and talent turned into superfluous objects. Yet against all odds, poetry circulates and is read. Rejecting the marketplace, costing almost nothing at all, it goes from mouth to mouth, like air and water. Its value and usefulness cannot be measured; a man rich in poetry may be a beggar. Nor can poems be hoarded: they must be spent. That is, they must be voiced. A great mystery: the poem contains poetry only if it doesn't keep it; the poetry must be given, shared, poured out like the wine from a bottle and water from a pitcher. All the arts, painting and sculpture in particular, being forms, are *things;* they can be kept, sold, and used as objects of financial speculation. Poetry, too, is a thing, but a thing that amounts to almost nothing: it is made of words, it is a puff of air that takes up no room in space. Unlike a painting, a poem shows no figures: it is a verbal incantation that provokes in the reader or hearer a spray of mental images. Poetry is heard with the ears but seen only with the mind. Its images are amphibious creatures: both forms and ideas, both sounds and silence.

According to everyone, we are witnessing today a great change. We do not know whether we are experiencing the end of modernity or its renewal. What will be the function of poetry this time around? If, as I hope and believe, a new form of political thought is coming into being, its creators will be obliged to listen to the *other* voice. That voice was not heeded by the revolutionary ideologues of our century, and this explains, in part at least, the cataclysmic failure of their plans. It would be disastrous if the new political philosophy were to ignore those realities that have been hidden and buried by the men and women of the Modern Age. The function of poetry for the last two hundred years has been to remind us of their existence; the poetry of tomorrow cannot do otherwise. Its mission will not be to provide new ideas but to announce what has been obstinately forgotten for centuries. Poetry is memory become image, and image become voice. The *other* voice is not the voice from beyond the grave: it is that of man fast asleep in the heart of hearts of mankind. It is a thousand years old and as old as you and I, and it has not yet been born. It is our grandfather, our brother, our great-grandchild.

We cannot know, of course, what direction the societies and the peoples of the twenty-first century will take.

Perhaps the new philosophy to answer the generous-hearted questions with which the Modern Age began is no more than a fond hope, a thing that might have been but was sidetracked forever by history. That would be terrible, for now in many parts of the world there are ominous signs of the return of old religious passions, nationalist fanaticisms, and worship of the tribe. Beliefs and passions that were suppressed by both liberal rationalism and regimes that flaunted the mask of "scientific socialism" are reappearing. They were deadly before and will become so once again if we cannot absorb or sublimate them.

No matter what the future holds in store for humanity, one thing seems certain to me: the institution of the market economy, in its heyday now, will change. It is not eternal; no human creation is. I do not know whether it will be modified by human wisdom or destroyed by its excesses and contradictions. In the latter case, it could drag democratic institutions down with it—a possibility that makes me tremble with fear, since we would then enter a dark age, as has happened more than once in history. The end of the Greco-Roman world, the decline of civilizations in India and China, the centuries of lethargy into which Islam fell. Whatever happens, it is clear that the immense, stupid, and suicidal waste of natural resources must come to an immediate end if the human species wishes to survive on this earth. The cause of the colossal squandering of riches—of our present and future life—is the circular process of the market. The market is highly efficient, but it has no goal; its sole purpose is to produce more in order to consume more. The obtuse economic policies of the governments of most under-developed countries, in Latin America, Asia, and Africa, have also contributed to the universal destruction and contamination of lakes, rivers, seas, valleys, forests, and mountains. No civilization of the past was ever ruled by such a blind, mechanical, destructive fatality.

The crisis, whatever our political and social institutions may be and independently of our beliefs and opinions, is already upon us, making itself felt in increasingly preemp-tory and threatening terms. It can even be said, without exaggeration, that the main theme of the last days of this century is not the political organization or reorganization of our societies, but the urgent question: How are we to ensure the survival of humanity? In the face of this reality, what can the function of poetry be? What does the *other* voice have to say? I argued, before, that if a new form of political thought were to emerge, the influence of poetry would be indirect: reminding us of certain buried realities, restoring them to life, presenting them. And confronted with the question of the survival of the human species on a poisoned and devastated planet, poetry can respond in no other way. Its influence must be indirect: intimating, suggesting, inspiring. Not logically demonstrating, but showing.

The operative mode of poetic thought is imagining, and imagination consists, essentially, of the ability to place contrary or divergent realities in relationship. All poetic forms and all linguistic figures have one thing in common: they seek, and often find, hidden resemblances. In the most extreme cases, they unite opposites. Comparisons, analogies, metaphors, metonymies, and the other devices of poetry—all tend to produce images in which this and that, the one and the other, the one and the many are joined. The poetic process conceives of language as an animated universe traversed by a dual current of attraction and repulsion. In language, the unions and the divisions, the love affairs and the separations of stars, cells, atoms, and men are reproduced. Each poem, whatever its subject and form and the ideas that shape it, is first and foremost a miniature animated cosmos. The poem unites the "ten thousand things that make up the universe," as the ancient Chinese put it.

Mirror of the fraternity of the cosmos, the poem is a model of what human society might be. In the face of the destruction of nature, it offers living proof of the brotherhood of the stars and elementary particles, of chemicals and consciousness. Poetry, exercising our imagination, teaches us to recognize differences and discover similarities. The universe is a live tissue of affinities and oppositions, and each poem is a practical lesson in harmony and concord, even when its subject is the wrath of the hero, the loneliness of an abandoned young girl, or the plunging of a mind into the still waters of the mirror. Poetry is the antidote to technology and the market. What poetry's function might be, in our time and in the time to come, is reduced to this. Nothing more than this? Nothing less.

The question posed at the beginning—How many and what kind of people read poems?—is inevitably bound up with the question of the survival of poetry in the modern world. And that question, in turn, is bound up with one of greater urgency and graver import: the survival of humanity itself. The poem, founded on the fraternity of the elements, forms, and creatures of the universe, is a model of survival. Hugo said it in a magnificent phrase: *Tout cherche tout, sans but, sans trêve, sans repos*—Everything seeks everything, without purpose, without end, without cease. The relationship between man and poetry is as old as our history: it began when human beings began to be human. The first hunters and gatherers looked at themselves in astonishment one day, for an interminable instant, in the still waters of a poem. Since that moment, people have not stopped looking at themselves in this mirror. And they have seen themselves, at one and the same time, as creators of images and as images of their creations. For that reason I can say,

with a modicum of certainty, that as long as there are
people, there will be poetry. The relationship, however,
may be broken. Born of the human imagination, it may die
if imagination dies or is corrupted. If human beings forget
poetry, they will forget themselves. And return to original
chaos.

MEXICO CITY, DECEMBER 1, 1989

Other books by Octavio Paz available
from Harcourt Brace Jovanovich, Publishers,
in Harvest/HBJ paperback editions

Convergences: Essays on Art and Literature
In Search of the Present: 1990 Nobel Lecture, bilingual edition
One Earth, Four or Five Worlds